Helping
Kids in
Crisis

Jo Hittner

Helping
Kids in
Crisis

Recognize • Respond • Refer

Jo Hittner, PhD

Saint Mary's Press®

Genuine recycled paper with 10% post-consumer waste.
5118400

The publishing team included Laurie Delgatto, development editor; Lorraine Kilmartin, reviewer; prepress and manufacturing coordinated by the prepublication and production services departments of Saint Mary's Press.

Jayne Stokke, cover illustration

Printed in the United States of America

Printing: 9 8 7 6 5 4 3 2 1

Year: 2014 13 12 11 10 09 08 07 06

ISBN-13: 978-0-88489-941-9
ISBN-10: 0-88489-941-1

Library of Congress Cataloging-in-Publication Data

Hittner, Jo Ann.
    Helping kids in crisis : recognize, respond, refer / Jo Ann Hittner.
    p. cm.
ISBN-13: 978-0-88489-941-9 (pbk.)
ISBN-10: 0-88489-941-1 (pbk.)
    1. Problem youth—Pastoral counseling of. I. Title.
BV4464.5.H58 2006
259'.2—dc22
                                                          2006012630

DEDICATION

To my husband, Leslie, whose support has given me the courage to accomplish seemingly impossible goals.

AUTHOR ACKNOWLEDGMENTS

I wish to thank Laurie Delgatto for her encouragement and editorial skills, which helped make this project a reality. And thanks to Brian Singer-Towns for asking me to think about writing this book and believing it was possible.

CONTENTS

INTRODUCTION

The ministry of pastoral care is an invitation to the ongoing process of caring deeply for young people, confronting them honestly when necessary, meeting them where they are, and showing them the rich possibilities of human wholeness. Pastoral care is an invitation to conversion in a holistic sense.

Pastoral care is also a ministry of compassionate and intrusive presence. We are challenged to surround young people with the best possible support systems; to connect young people with a web of family, youth ministers, teachers, and significant adults; and to be a compassionate presence in their lives. Our presence is intrusive when necessary. We challenge and confront negative or harmful behaviors, values, and attitudes, and we witness to Gospel values and lifestyles.

Though pastoral care is much broader than dealing with crises, responding to young people experiencing distress or engaging in risky behaviors is an important aspect of pastoral care. It is essential to remember, however, the difference between counseling and responding. Counseling requires a specific set of skills, training, and expertise. Most of those who minister with youth are not trained as counselors.

Yet most adults working with young people can still effectively respond in crises by developing the recognition, response, and referral skills needed to provide caring support to young people when necessary. Recognition skills simply refer to one's ability to see the behavioral signs indicating an individual or group is in crisis. Response skills mean actually reaching out to and making contact with an individual or group in crisis, and referral skills include acknowledging that an issue requires a more professional response and identifying potential resources. Adults can indeed be pastoral responders and caregivers.

This means each of us who work with young people (pastors, coordinators of youth ministry, pastoral associates, ministry leaders, catechists, teachers, and other caregivers) must be knowledgeable about the varieties of issues potentially present in the lives of the young people and families in our care. When a young person's difficulties are beyond the realm of our own credentials and experience, each of us has a responsibility to connect the young person or family with someone who is trained in the skills of intervention, diagnosis, and counseling.

Helping Kids in Crisis identifies more than thirty of the most common pastoral care issues today's young people face. Each chapter provides illustrative cases, a list of signs and symptoms, and suggestions as to when and from whom to seek additional professional help. The chapters deal with such issues as addictions, behavioral and mental disorders, bereavement, suicide, divorce, violence, and abuse. Each chapter also includes practical ideas for adding pastoral care strategies to existing ministry programs as well as recommended resources for further study. As ministry leaders, each of us is likely to encounter serious situations and moments of crisis in the lives of the youth and families with whom we minister. *Helping Kids in Crisis* was written for precisely that reason.

SECTION ONE
ADDICTIONS

Addiction is "a compulsive need for and use of a habit-forming substance, characterized by tolerance and by well-defined physiological symptoms upon withdrawal" (*Webster's Collegiate Dictionary*, p. 14). This definition limits addictions to substances such as alcohol, nicotine, cocaine, and other drugs. It does not include obsessive gambling, video gaming, and sexual activity. However, the definition of *addict* includes "to devote or surrender (oneself) to something habitually or obsessively" (p. 14). These latter examples fit addictive behaviors because the person addicted has physiological symptoms when he attempts to quit and also experiences tolerance effects; that is, at first small amounts of the behavior satisfy, but as time goes on, more experiences are needed to provide satisfaction.

Possible types of addictions include abuse of substances such as alcohol, nicotine, marijuana, depressants such as barbiturates and tranquilizers, stimulants such as inhalants and prescription drugs sold or exchanged without permission, heroin, hallucinogens, methamphetamine, and steroids. Gambling addictions, sexual addictions, and video gaming addictions can be added to the list.

1
SUBSTANCE ABUSE

Substance abuse starts when a young person makes a conscious decision to use drugs or alcohol. Used too often, drugs may cause a young person to crave the substance. That's because physical changes take place in the brain. Neurons, or brain cells, use chemical messengers called neurotransmitters to "talk" to one another. Drugs interfere with this process by making structural changes in brain cells. Mood, memory, thinking, and even motor skills such as walking may be affected. Not everyone becomes addicted. But any drug abuse is dangerous.

Young people's brains and bodies are still developing. Drug abuse and addiction interfere with young people's sense of who they are and how they learn and mature. These problems can harm a young person's future—physically, emotionally, and behaviorally—even leading to depression and anxiety. Drugs can weaken one's ability to concentrate and store information. Being under the influence of drugs can also impair judgment, leading to risky decisions about sex or about getting into a car with someone who is also under the influence.

Using alcohol and tobacco at a young age increases the risk of using other drugs later. Some young people will experiment and stop, or continue to use occasionally, without significant problems. Others will develop a dependency, moving on to more dangerous drugs and causing significant harm to themselves and possibly others.

Case Study

Patrick is sixteen. He comes to youth activities with an unusual amount of nonchalance. He is not interested in what is going on and doesn't seem to care that he is not involved. When asked about his interests, he says he doesn't have any in particular. He does not seem depressed, just uninterested. He used to be interested, involved, and enthusiastic. He does not make eye contact when others comment that he seems different from his typical self. His usual friends are avoiding him, and he is hanging around with a different group of friends. These new friends have been on the periphery previously, and now Patrick seems to be comfortable there as well. At times he doesn't seem to retain any information, and at other times he seems giddy and not able to think through problems.

Signs and Symptoms

Typically, abuse of a substance is a "maladaptive pattern of substance use leading to clinically significant impairment or distress . . . occurring within a 12-month period" (DSM-IV-TR, *Diagnostic and Statistical Manual of Mental Disorders,* p. 199). This means that a person who uses drugs periodically for a short time may not be making wise decisions and may be abusing a substance, but he will likely not be diagnosed with substance abuse or dependency. However, once a line is crossed where problems begin to occur, such as inability to function, placing oneself in dangerous situations, or getting into legal problems, abuse is probably present. Dependency is a more pervasive use of the substance without concern for consequences, including physical symptoms, financial ruin, or deterioration of relationships.

Symptoms of substance abuse always include recurrent use and may also include these characteristics:

- sudden personality changes, including abrupt changes in work or school attendance, quality of work, work output, grades, discipline
- unusual flare-ups or outbreaks of temper
- not fulfilling obligations at work or school
- operating a motor vehicle while under the influence of any addictive substance
- getting into legal difficulties for any reason, including inappropriate behavior such as disorderly conduct, theft, and sexual improprieties
- general changes in overall attitude
- loss of interest in favorite hobbies and pursuits
- changes in friendships, reluctance to talk about friends or have them visit
- difficulty in concentration, paying attention
- sudden jitteriness, nervousness, or aggression
- deterioration of physical appearance and grooming
- change in appetite, weight loss or gain
- wearing of sunglasses at inappropriate times
- continual wearing of long-sleeved garments, particularly in hot weather, or reluctance to wear short-sleeved attire when appropriate
- association with known substance abusers
- unusual borrowing of money from friends, coworkers, or parents
- theft of small items from employer, home, or school
- secretive behavior regarding actions and possessions; poorly concealed attempts to avoid attention and suspicion, such as frequent trips to storage rooms, restrooms, basements, and so on

Different substances lend themselves to different groups of symptoms. The most glaring symptom in all cases is a change — sometimes radical — in behavior.

Causes of addiction vary from individual to individual. Some people can use chemicals repeatedly and not get addicted until later.

Others, however, can use a chemical once and become addicted. Some of this is due to metabolism, genetic predisposition, and other biological factors. All illegal drugs are potentially addictive. Drugs work to change the brain chemistry and tap into the pleasurable feelings we all desire. However, drugs come with a high price; they damage the body and stunt emotional growth, making it hard to handle daily stresses and solve everyday problems.

Response, Diagnosis, and Treatment

With any addiction, denial is the norm. It is easy for someone to say, "I am not addicted; I can quit anytime." It is easy to say as well, "Everyone else does it, and I am not using as much as they are." Neither of these statements makes any difference when the person is experiencing negative consequences from his use of the drugs. Directly confronting youth with observations about their behavior, their choices, and the consequences of their behavior and choices works well in the beginning stages of use. However, this is rarely effective once the young person is well established in his patterns of use.

If the young person is not willing to look at his use, an intervention of some sort is needed. Parental contact is essential. If you are concerned but the parents are not, very little (if anything) can be done, but sharing your concerns may stimulate their thinking process. Parental permission is needed for the young person to seek help in most instances. Youth can legally get a chemical dependency evaluation on their own, and the information cannot be shared with their parents. However, they would have to pay for it themselves or have access to their parents' health insurance information. This rarely happens.

Thankfully, most of the time parents *are* concerned, and with their leadership, change can occur. Parents need to make contact with a chemical dependency counselor, who will conduct an assessment of the young person's chemical use and make recommendations. The counselor will determine if the use is at an abusive or addictive level and recommend further treatment or reduction of use. If treatment is recommended, the counselor will help the family find outpatient treatment in which the young person attends sessions but remains at home. If the problem is serious enough, the counselor might recommend inpatient treatment in which the young person is placed in a treatment center without going home until treatment is concluded. This option is more intense than outpatient treatment and is shorter in duration.

Many methods are used to determine substance use; among them is urine or blood testing. Another method is by interviewing parents, teachers, and other caregivers regarding the history of the patient and the patient's current behavioral aspects.

A major difficulty in making a diagnosis is the consideration of dual diagnoses. A dual diagnosis is given to any person who has both a substance abuse problem and an emotional or psychiatric disorder. For the patient to fully recover, he must be treated for both problems.

Drug addiction is treated by having the person withdraw from the drug. Treatment consists of looking at the underlying cause for the use of the drug. If it is a mental health issue, mental health therapy might be recommended in addition to the substance abuse treatment. If a physical problem is present, referral to a physician is recommended. If the issue is connections with other drug users, a recommendation is made for a change in friends. This is done in a supportive way to encourage finding friends who are not using drugs. This is important because the pressure to resume using will be too great to ignore once treatment is complete. Treatment also involves looking at alternatives to drug use to get one's emotional needs met.

Aftercare is usually a part of treatment whereby the person is expected to continue to see a counselor and other group members for a period of time to gain support for remaining abstinent from the drug. A twelve-step program such as Alcoholics Anonymous (AA) or Narcotics Anonymous (NA) or another support network is usually recommended to maintain sobriety or abstinence. Relapse (using again) happens with some frequency, and this is dealt with either by gaining more support or by repeating the treatment program.

Pastoral Care Strategies

In your own ministry to and with young people, keep these strategies in mind:

- Be a good role model.
- Promote healthy choices and avoidance of all illegal drugs.
- Understand that addictions are not changed by willpower but require professional intervention.
- Contact parents when adolescents seem to be having problems with alcohol or other drugs.
- Support professional counseling when drugs are being abused.
- Provide substance abuse education to young people and parents.
- Connect parents and young people with already existing education programs.
- Allow AA or NA to meet in your church facilities.
- Start an AA, NA, or other support group chapter in your parish, with the assistance of a professional.
- Create a binder of current resources (mental health professionals, abuse counselors, treatment facilities, and so on).

Recommended Reading

- *Choices and Consequences: What to Do When a Teenager Uses Alcohol/ Drugs,* by Dick Shaefer (Center City, MN: Hazelden Foundation, 1998).
- *Dirty: A Search for Answers Inside America's Teenage Drug Epidemic,* by Meredith Maran (New York: HarperSanFrancisco, 2003).
- *Helping Your Chemically Dependent Teenager Recover: A Guide for Parents and Other Concerned Adults,* by Peter Cohen (Center City, MN: Hazelden Foundation, 1998).
- *Teens Under the Influence: The Truth About Kids, Alcohol, and Other Drugs – How to Recognize the Problem and What to Do About It,* by Katherine Ketcham (New York: Ballantine Books, 2003).

2
GAMBLING ADDICTIONS

Gambling has recently increased in popularity among adolescents as more gambling opportunities have become available to the adult population. Gambling is the act of risking money or something else of value on an activity with an uncertain outcome. Playing cards or video games for money, buying raffle tickets, betting on who's going to win the next game of pool, or wagering a favorite CD on the outcome of a sports event — these are all gambling.

For most people, gambling is an activity that is fun and entertaining — one that can be experienced with little or no harmful effects. For others gambling can be a serious problem that continues even after the fun is gone.

Problem gambling is a progressive behavioral disorder in which an individual has a psychologically uncontrollable urge to gamble. This results in excessive gambling, the outcome of which is the loss of time, money, and self-esteem. The gambling reaches a point where it compromises, disrupts, and ultimately destroys the gambler's personal life and relationships. Just as some people become addicted to drugs or alcohol, it is possible for a person to become obsessed with an uncontrollable urge to gamble. The effects of this addiction are much greater than the obvious financial losses that usually result from repeated gambling. The long-term result is a steady deterioration of the mental and physical health of both the gambler and his family.

Teens often begin gambling with adults and progress into independent gambling over time. Adolescents are more vulnerable to gambling problems when their parents or other significant people in their life gamble. They also are more vulnerable when they are lonely, have poor self-esteem, or want to escape from the reality around them.

Case Study

Mark is interested in various projects and activities. He is usually excited about a lot of things. He seems to be somewhat of a risk taker, but at sixteen he is comparable to a lot of his peers. He enjoys competition and wants to win at almost any cost. He has been more jittery and anxious lately, and he doesn't seem to be as interested in what his friends are doing or in spending time with them. He used to play a number of sports but has become almost exclusively interested in following the NFL, paying close attention to which teams are in the running for the Super Bowl. In fact, he seems to have an almost obsessive interest in who is winning. It started innocently enough with getting involved with sports pools. After all, Mark thought, what could be the harm in placing bets on teams he knew would win? He had all the information he needed to make a wise choice, and most of the time he has been right. Occasionally he has gotten overconfident and spent more money than he intended. This has caused him to lose more money than he actually has, and so he simply borrows money from his friends, who seem to be willing enough to lend it to him, at least for now. Mark also believes that the longer he gambles the more money he'll make. All he has to do to make up for his losses is to play "one more time," and he is sure he will win big and be able to pay back the money he borrowed plus enough to buy things he wants for himself. Just one more game, one more win, one more chance.

Signs and Symptoms

Research suggests that most young people gamble because of the excitement it generates as well as the escape from problems it provides. Gambling becomes a way of dealing with stress and can be reinforcing. Gambling has the same effect as drug addiction of connecting with the pleasure-seeking part of the brain and creating a high. Anyone who gambles can develop a gambling problem. If gambling is a frequent activity in the home or among friends, young people are at greater risk for developing a problem with gambling. Often young people with gambling problems have troubles in other areas of their life they need to sort out, such as feeling lonely or arguing a lot with their parents. Sometimes referred to as the "hidden addiction," problem gambling is not as easily detected as alcoholism or substance abuse. But these warning signs may indicate a person is crossing the line into addiction:

- having unexplained amounts of money
- skipping classes
- missing work
- frequently borrowing money from friends and family members
- feeling restless or irritable when not able to gamble
- becoming preoccupied with gambling
- continuing to gamble despite significant losses
- feeling helpless and depressed or having thoughts of suicide

Adolescents are more likely to be addicted to gambling than adults. This is probably owing to their inability to foresee consequences of their behavior, their impulsiveness, and their feelings of invulnerability. Males are more likely than females to have gambling addictions. Risk factors for young people include not feeling like they belong to a group of friends, having role models who gamble, and having low self-esteem and unresolved issues from which they want to escape.

People with one addiction are more at risk to develop another. Some problem gamblers also find they have a problem with alcohol or drugs. Some problem gamblers never experience any other addiction because no other substance or activity gives them the same feeling as gambling does.

Response, Diagnosis, and Treatment

A gambling addiction is progressive. In most people it begins slowly and grows until the gambler's life becomes increasingly unmanageable. As repeated efforts to gain control over the addiction fail, life for the compulsive gambler begins to fall apart. If the compulsive gambler could stop chasing losses, he would. All compulsive gamblers can stop gambling for a while. But most people need professional help to stop for life.

It is not always easy to recognize a teenager with a gambling problem. However, some of the most obvious warning signs are financial problems. In addition, gambling teens usually let their schoolwork slide, miss classes, and don't stay focused. Gamblers go through a phase where they feel lucky and special, followed by a downward spiral ending in a desperation phase where they can't stop gambling.

Professionals working with a gambling addict must look at the young person's attitudes toward gambling. Therapists must also make collateral contact with family members or friends who are familiar with the young person's choices. Collateral contact means that other people are consulted as a means of confirming (or refuting) the person's comments.

Treatment consists of inpatient or outpatient therapy. A severe addiction may require a more intensive inpatient therapy. A less severe addiction or abuse might merit outpatient treatment.

Recovery is a process of learning how to resist the gambling urge, developing healthy coping skills, and taking responsibility for past behavior by making appropriate financial restitution or personal amends to those who may have suffered as a result. Outpatient therapy often involves a series of therapy sessions. Therapy addresses underlying personal and social issues and encourages the development of healthy coping styles. Instead of avoiding issues, youth are empowered to deal effectively with their problems through socially acceptable strategies. Individuals with gambling problems are also encouraged to engage in healthier activities. Family members often play an important role in outpatient rehabilitation. Family members typically attend a separate counseling session where they learn what compulsive gambling is and how they can support their family member's recovery.

Refraining from any forms of gambling and changing friends so the temptation to return to gambling is minimized are also part of the treatment. An aftercare program to maintain the gains and prevent relapse are usually included as well.

Whatever the situation, problem gamblers can recover to lead happier, more productive lives than they may have experienced even before their gambling.

Pastoral Care Strategies

It is extremely important when working with youth to be appropriate role models for them. They look to the adults in their life for direction, guidance, and support. Minimizing problems that are budding or progressing more rapidly than expected is not helpful. Young people need to be confronted with their choices, helped to see the consequences of those choices, and given guidance on how to make better choices. Supporting youth while letting them know about the consequences of their behaviors is critical to keeping their trust.

In your own ministry to and with young people, keep these strategies in mind:

- Pay attention to seemingly insignificant changes in the attitudes and behaviors of the young people you serve.
- Support professional counseling when gambling problems are evident.
- Provide gambling addiction education to young people and parents.
- Connect parents and young people to already existing education programs.
- Refer any youth and their parents with concerns to the national gambling hotlines.

- Allow Gamblers Anonymous groups to meet in churches or local schools.
- Begin a Gamblers Anonymous group for young people in the area.
- Research and write an article on teen gambling for the parish bulletin or local newspaper.
- Develop a display highlighting the issues around problem gambling.
- Work with local schools to develop gambling prevention programs.

Recommended Reading

- *Gambling and Gaming Addictions in Adolescence: Parent, Adolescent and Child Training Skills,* by Mark Griffiths (Boston: Blackwell Publishing, 2002).
- *This Must Be Hell: A Look at Pathological Gambling,* by Humphrey Hale (Lincoln, NE: Writers Club Press, 2000).
- *Wanna Bet? Everything You Wanted to Know About Teen Gambling but Never Thought to Ask,* by the North American Training Institute (Duluth, MN: North American Training Institute, 1997).

3
SEXUAL ADDICTIONS

Sexual addiction is defined as any sexually related, compulsive behavior that interferes with normal living. Sexual addiction is also known as sexual dependency and sexual compulsivity. By any name, it is a compulsive behavior that completely dominates the addict's life. Sexual addicts make sex a higher priority than any other aspect of life.

Sexual addiction can be understood by comparing it to other types of addictions. Individuals addicted to alcohol or other drugs, for example, develop a relationship with their "chemical(s) of choice" — a relationship that takes precedence over any and all other aspects of their lives. Addicts find they need drugs simply to feel "normal."

In sexual addiction, a parallel situation exists. Sex—like food or drugs in other addictions—provides the "high," and addicts become dependent on this sexual high to feel normal. They substitute unhealthy relationships for healthy ones. They opt for temporary pleasure rather than the deeper qualities of truly intimate relationships.

The tendency to deny problematic behaviors around sexual activity is high because of the societal taboos and privacy of sexual acts. As with all addictions, the repeated inability to control the behavior, heightened tension before the behavior, pleasure during the behavior, and the necessity of increasing the behavior to obtain satisfaction apply with sexual addiction as well.

Case Study

Mavis is an attractive, seemingly well liked fifteen-year-old girl. She has a reputation of being fun, is willing to take risks, and enjoys being around boys. She talks about a variety of activities but focuses most on her relationships with boys. She has struggled with drug abuse and seems to have conquered that problem. But something does not seem right about her preoccupation with hugging, holding hands, and being in physical contact with the male gender. Mavis does not have the same boyfriend for any length of time and has a reputation for being "easy."

Mavis comes from a two-parent home, and her parents' marriage is considered happy. Her siblings are well known and well liked by everyone. Her parents are involved in the community; both are working professionals and strong supporters of school athletics. Mavis is not as athletic as her siblings and appears to be somewhat isolated from them. She is a good student, however, and makes up for her lack of athletic ability with strong academic skills. The interesting thing about her is that she is such an ordinary girl from a "good family." Lately she seems excluded from her family and spends most her time and energy seeking attention from boys. Her parents do not seem to notice or do not seem concerned if they do notice. No one is apparently commenting on her isolation, lack of connection with her family, and her promiscuity—perhaps because she is well liked, perhaps because it seems normal. Mavis feels like her life is out of control, and she is not feeling good about who she is or what she is doing.

Signs and Symptoms

No single behavior pattern defines sexual addiction. Individual behaviors may not indicate a problem, but a cumulative effect may indicate something is awry and that the behaviors or attitudes are outside the norm of adolescent behaviors. Sexual addiction is often progressive. Although a young person with a sexual addiction may be able to control herself for a time, inevitably her addictive behaviors will return and quickly escalate to previous levels and beyond. Some people with this addiction begin adding additional acting-out behaviors.

Young people with a sexual addiction may display these characteristics:

- interest in pornography (magazines, books, Internet sites)
- violation of others' body space
- exhibitionism, voyeurism, and obscene gestures, along with indecent exposure and indecent phone calls
- sexual preoccupation or anxiety that interferes with daily functioning
- indiscriminate sexual contact with more than one partner during the same period of time
- sexually aggressive ideas or obscenities that embarrass others
- sexual graffiti, especially when it is chronic and impacts individuals
- compulsive masturbation
- self- or other-degrading or humiliating comments with a sexual theme
- sexually explicit conversations with significantly younger children

(Based on Focus Adolescent Services, "The Range of Teenage Sexual Behavior")

Sexual addicts experience intense mood shifts, often owing to the despair and shame of having unwanted sex. Sexual addicts are caught in a crushing cycle of shame-driven and shame-creating behavior. Although shame drives the sexual addicts' actions, it also becomes the unwanted consequence of a euphoric escape into sex.

The likelihood of a young person having a sexual addiction increases with personal experience of sexual abuse; rigid, emotionally disengaged family members; sexual exposure at a young age; or living in a family with chemical addiction or other addictive patterns.

Response, Diagnosis, and Treatment

Sexual addiction is not about repeated sexual activity but rather is primarily an addiction expressed in sexual activity. Often people suffering from sexual addictions don't know what is wrong with them. They may suffer from clinical depression or have suicidal tendencies. They may even think they are losing their mind. However, recognizable behavior patterns indicate the presence of sexual addiction.

Many sources of help are available to provide information, support, and assistance for sexual addicts trying to regain control of their life. These include inpatient and outpatient treatment, professional associations, self-help groups, and aftercare support groups. Treatment programs also offer family counseling programs, support groups, and educational workshops for addicts and their families to help them understand how their beliefs and family life relate to the addiction.

Diagnosis should be done by a mental health professional. Diagnosis is based on questions related to ability to terminate the activity voluntarily, legal difficulties involved, interference of daily functioning, information gathered from others who would know the person's attitudes and behaviors, and motivation to change. Treatment is similar to other addictions; that is, the person will need to recognize triggers to the addictive behaviors, stop associating with people who also engage in the behaviors, and refrain from, or at least significantly decrease, the activities.

For example, if the person visits pornographic or sexually explicit Internet sites, she will need to contract to stop using those sites. If masturbation is part of the addiction, the person will have to contract to refrain from that behavior. Twelve-step programs such as Sex Addicts Anonymous are excellent support networks. Monitoring behaviors and attitudes and dealing with underlying issues such as sexual abuse or early sexual exposure might be part of the treatment program as well.

Recovery is possible, and life has joyful potential. With recovery, life is no longer depleting, but replenishing; not secret, but open; not isolating, but loving. Like other types of addiction, sexual addiction may never be "cured." However, individuals can achieve a state of recovery. Maintaining that recovery can be a lifelong, day-by-day process. A good approach teaches the addict to take her recovery one day at a time—concentrating on the present, not the future.

Pastoral Care Strategies

In your own ministry to and with young people, keep these strategies in mind:

- Have a respectful attitude regarding your own sexuality.
- Role model healthy sexual behaviors.
- Set appropriate boundaries with the youth, especially in the area of physical contact.
- Provide a supportive environment for discussion of sexual issues.
- Obtain information to share with youth in a nonthreatening manner regarding resources for information on sexual issues.
- Confront issues that are problematic in an empathic, understanding, straightforward manner to reduce shame, guilt, and nondisclosure.
- Provide adequate (church-approved) sexuality programs for young people and their parents.
- Encourage parents to re-evaluate the types and amounts of media they allow in the home.

Recommended Reading

- *Don't Call It Love: Recovery from Sexual Addiction,* by Patrick Carnes (New York: Bantam Books, 2002).
- *Out of the Shadows: Understanding Sexual Addiction,* by Patrick Carnes (Center City, MN: Hazelden Foundation, 2001).

4
COMPUTER AND VIDEO GAME ADDICTIONS

With the advent of computers, video games, and the Internet, the interest in playing games on the computer, television, or handheld devices has increased exponentially. Most children and adolescents are able to pursue their interests in video games without any problems. However, some experience a "rush" that is similar to that of people on amphetamines. For these young people, being unable to play a video game is akin to not having access to a drug. They are willing to forego their responsibilities to play, and they experience withdrawal when they are not playing.

Video game addiction is the use of computers and video games to change an individual's mood. Use becomes abuse when it interferes with one's work or school, disrupts personal and family relationships, and becomes increasingly necessary for one to feel good.

Case Study

Steve began playing video games with his dad at about age eight. The two of them would spend hours together trying to get to the next level or trying to outdo the other. Now that Steve is fourteen, he plays on his own. He has frequently stayed up nearly all night playing. If his friends want to play video games, he is more than happy to join them. If they want to do something else, he declines. His grades have taken a nosedive because he is no longer interested in doing his homework. His parents cannot get him to do any chores at home; he is always playing video games. He has been having some difficulty staying awake in class and has been known to miss class sometimes because he has stayed up all night or does not have his homework done. He used to be involved in outside activities but has pretty much dropped out of everything. When he is not involved in a video game, he is irritable and not enjoyable to be around. The only friends he has now are those who are also avid players of video games. His parents and former friends are concerned, but apart from forbidding him to play video games, they are out of ideas. Steve has such horrible reactions to anyone who suggests he cut back or not play games that no one thinks it is worth the hassle. They hope he gets over this phase and returns to his old self soon.

Signs and Symptoms

Having an addiction to playing video games is not dissimilar to having an addiction to drugs or alcohol. The symptoms fit the criteria for an addiction in the *Diagnostic and Statistical Manual of Mental Disorders* (DSM-IV-TR). The difference is that legal difficulties are not usually involved unless the person starts being truant from school on a regular basis. Young people with an addiction to video games may exhibit the following symptoms:

- withdrawing from friends and family to play games
- neglecting schoolwork or other responsibilities in order to play
- lying about how much time is spent playing
- having temper tantrums when time for playing is limited
- repeatedly breaking family rules about when and how much playing time is allowed
- falling asleep in school
- having failing grades

- using the computer or playing video games instead of being with friends
- feeling irritable when not playing video games
- dropping out of previously enjoyed social groups
- spending most nonschool time playing video games
- feeling a sense of well-being or euphoria while gaming
- being unable to stop the activity

Social pressure or a lack of social skills can lead to video game addiction. Video gaming allows a young person to escape various problems, including stress; loneliness; feelings of isolation, rejection, or not belonging; lack of self-confidence; or depression. Not surprisingly there is some relationship between video game addiction and violence. This seems to be most prevalent when the video games are violent themselves. Because the player is the actor in the games, which is a virtual world, he is likely to become less sensitive to violence in the real world. The ability of the brain to reinforce positive experiences contributes to the addiction factor in video gaming. The exact number of young people addicted to video gaming is not known. What is known is that more youth are spending more time gaming. The games are getting more complex, and although they are being rated for violent and sexual content, young people are finding ways to access them more frequently.

Response, Diagnosis, and Treatment

To connect with youth who might be addicted to video games, it is important for them to believe you have their best interests in mind. This is not easy with an addiction, and because video gaming is done privately and has few physical consequences, it becomes challenging. However, sharing your concerns directly and calmly will help. Provide specific examples of negative consequences, such as poor grades, sleepiness, and poor sociability. Talk to the youth without arguing or threatening. Suggest specific changes. Inform the parents of your concerns, using specific examples and current consequences.

Encourage the parents to seek professional help for their child if other strategies have failed and the gaming continues unabated.

Video gaming addiction is a relatively new phenomenon, and although treatment centers are beginning to be developed, very few are available. Outpatient treatment for addictive behaviors is the usual course of action. This consists of an interview by an addiction counselor, who determines the extent of the addiction. The basic approach in treatment is to teach the young person how to normalize his behavior. Recommendations would be based on the consequences of the behavior. For example, if the youth is unable to manage his behavior, grades are changing in a negative direction, isolation and aggression are present, then the recommendation might be to remove all gaming materials from the youth. This would be similar to the youth addicted to alcohol or drugs. If the problem is not so severe, recommendations might be made to limit gaming time. If this does not work and the gaming continues with negative consequences, the recommendation might again be to remove gaming devices. Because video gaming is a nonessential activity, total removal of the source of addiction is possible.

Pastoral Care Strategies

Spending time in meaningful activities benefits everyone. Taking advantage of the opportunity to play together is one of the most wholesome activities available to both youth and adults. In your own ministry to and with young people, keep these strategies in mind:

- Encourage other activities besides video games even when video games are popular in the group.
- Sponsor speakers on the positive and negative attributes of video gaming.
- Stay informed about issues concerning video gaming in your area.
- Be alert to youth who may need help limiting their time or access to video games, and help them keep their resolve to stay within their limits.

- Provide media literacy workshops for young people to explore the issues surrounding violent video games.
- "Reinvent" a violent video game with young people—propose peaceful characters and actions. Encourage young people to write to Nintendo, Sega, or Genesis with a new game idea.
- Encourage legislation to limit the sale of adult games to minors.

Recommended Reading

- *Caught in the Net: How to Recognize the Signs of Internet Addiction — and a Winning Strategy for Recovery,* by Kimberly S. Young (Hoboken, NJ: Wiley Publishers, 1998).
- *Gambling and Gaming Addictions in Adolescence: Parent, Adolescent and Child Training Skills,* by Mark Griffiths (Boston: Blackwell Publishing, 2002).
- *Virtual Addiction: Help for Netheads, Cyberfreaks, and Those Who Love Them,* by David N. Greenfield (Oakland, CA: New Harbinger Publications, 1999).

Section Two
VIOLENCE

Violence is a term connoting fear, terror, abuse, and harm. Violence encompasses a range of behaviors including the intentional use of physical force or power—threatened or actual—against oneself, another person, or against a group or community. Violence has a high likelihood of resulting in injury, death, psychological harm, and deprivation. Violence can also involve witnessing the harm of others.

Along with neglect, abuse of any form is seen as violent, including harassment, verbal sexual innuendoes, and threats of physical harm.

5
CHILD NEGLECT

Child neglect can be defined as willfully failing to provide for a child's basic necessities of life, such as food, clothing, shelter, and medical care, or failing to provide guidance and supervision. Essentially neglect involves an ongoing pattern of inadequate care.

According to many experts, neglect is a greater social threat than active abuse. More than half the investigated incidents of maltreatment involve neglect. Many neglected children and adolescents seem to be harmed just as severely as victims of more active sorts of abuse. Indifference, forgotten promises, and withdrawal are all inappropriate and harmful behaviors; they damage children and teenagers who may feel they are not worth their parents' concern and care.

Neglect is more commonly reported with young children, but adolescents can also be victims. Types of neglect include physical, educational, emotional, or medical. School personnel are the most likely to notice neglect because of poor hygiene, severe weight gain or loss, inadequate medical care, or frequent absences from school.

Physical neglect is the most commonly reported type of maltreatment among children. It includes the refusal or extreme delay in obtaining necessary health care; rejection of a child resulting in her being expelled from home; not adequately providing for the youth's safety and physical needs; or abandonment.

Educational neglect occurs when parents allow chronic truancy, do not permit special education when required, or do not enroll the youth in school when she is of mandatory school age.

Emotional neglect includes a child witnessing spousal abuse; allowing a child to use drugs or alcohol; refusing or failing to provide necessary psychological care; withholding of affection; or constant belittling of the youth.

Medical neglect is the failure to provide adequate medical care when the ability to do so is available. Medical neglect can result in overall poor health and medical problems that are compounded over time.

Case Study

At age fourteen, Stacy was recognized by everyone around her as someone who did not smell good, dress appropriately, or seem to have friends. She was not invited over to anyone's home and did not have anyone come to her home. It was common knowledge that her parents were heavy drinkers, and it was suspected that Stacy was allowed to drink with her parents. She was not easy to be around because she was dirty and unkempt and had a nasty body odor. She had not been in the community for long. It seemed she moved frequently. Not much was known about her parents except that they did not participate in adult-sponsored activities. They too were unkempt and ill-mannered. Stacy tried to participate in activities, but she appeared tired, noncommunicative, and isolated. It was thought she might be coming to programs because food was present, rather than because she wanted to participate. She was seemingly hungry all the time. When asked about her well-being, she would shrug her shoulders and not say anything except she was fine and really didn't want to talk about it. Her parents did not return phone calls when teachers and other concerned adults wanted to talk to them about Stacy. And Stacy's parents were known to offer only negative comments about Stacy when they were in public. Stacy commented that she was unwilling to tell her parents anything because they would not listen to her and said she was a liar so why should they bother.

Signs and Symptoms

Most parents don't hurt or neglect their children intentionally. Many were themselves abused or neglected as children. Very young or inexperienced parents might not know how to take care of children or what they can reasonably expect from children at different stages of development. Circumstances that place families under extraordinary stress—for instance, poverty, divorce, sickness, disability— sometimes take their toll in child maltreatment. Parents who abuse alcohol or other drugs are more likely to abuse or neglect their children.

Child neglect is usually quite obvious and easy to detect, but it may be difficult to prove. This is because neglect is often paired with poverty, and the criteria of lack of willingness versus the inability to provide for the youth are often debatable.

Victims of neglect may exhibit these symptoms:
- dirty skin and an offensive body odor
- unwashed, uncombed hair
- tattered, poorly fitting, and unclean clothing as well as clothing that is inappropriate to the weather or the situation
- frequently left unsupervised or alone for periods of time that are not age-appropriate
- physical conditions and complaints and illnesses not responded to by parent(s)
- frequent hunger or begging for or stealing food
- gorging self, eating in large gulps
- early arrival to school, reluctance to go home
- cruelty to classmates

- frequent school absences or tardiness
- severe developmental lags (speech, motor, sensory) without an obvious physical cause
- lack of attachment to parents

Sometimes neglect is associated with poverty. However, neglect is actually the refusal, rather than the inability, to provide for the needs of the children. When basic needs are not routinely met because of parental (or caretaker) refusal, children often view the world as a dangerous and unsafe place where adults cannot be trusted to take care of them.

Response, Diagnosis, and Treatment

If you suspect neglect, reporting it can protect the child and get help for the family. Each state identifies mandatory reporters (groups of people who are required to report suspicions of child abuse or neglect). Church workers, teachers, and any professionals who work directly with young people are mandated reporters. However, any concerned person can and should report suspected child abuse or neglect. A report is not an accusation; it is an expression of concern and a request for an investigation or evaluation of the child's situation. If you suspect a child is in a dangerous situation, take immediate action.

Your suspicion of child abuse or neglect is enough to make a report. You are not required to provide proof. Investigators in your community will make the determination of whether abuse or neglect has occurred. Almost every state has a law to protect from prosecution or liability people who make good-faith reports of child abuse.

A report of possible child maltreatment will first be screened by hotline staff or a social worker. If the worker feels there is enough credible information to indicate neglect may have occurred or is at risk of occurring, a report will be referred to staff, who will conduct an investigation. Investigators respond within a particular time period (anywhere from a few hours to a few days), depending on the potential severity of the situation. They may speak with the child, the parents, and other people in contact with the child (such as doctors, teachers, or child care providers). Their purpose is to determine if abuse or neglect has occurred and if it is likely to happen again. If the investigator finds that no abuse or neglect has occurred, or what happened does not meet the state's definition of abuse or neglect, the case will be closed and the family may or may not be referred elsewhere for services.

If the investigator thinks the child is at risk of harm, the family may be referred to services to reduce the risk of future maltreatment. These may include mental health care, medical care, parenting skills classes, employment assistance, and concrete support, such as financial or housing assistance. In some cases where the child's safety cannot be ensured, the child may be removed from the home.

Pastoral Care Strategies

Adults who work with children in situations of neglect need to keep in mind they cannot totally "rescue" these children. Giving them what is physically lacking in their lives may be a first response, but making the necessary reports is critical for the children to receive long-term adequate care. In your own ministry to and with young people, keep these strategies in mind:

- Remember that all church, school, medical personnel, and staff members of youth-serving organizations are mandated to report suspicion of child neglect.
- Always be gentle, understanding, and accepting of all young people, regardless of their circumstances at home.
- Never comment on a young person's appearance or attire ("You can't come in here dressed like that!")
- Provide classes on parenting in stressful situations.
- Begin a support group such as Parents Anonymous in your area for parents who are having difficulties with their children.
- Inform parents about services available in the community for low-income families.

- Help a family under stress. If a family you know seems to be in crisis or under stress, offer to help babysit, help with chores and errands, or suggest resources in the community that can assist the family, such as faith community leaders, teachers, and doctors.
- Help local organizations distribute educational materials on positive parenting and child abuse prevention.
- Mentor parents in programs that match experienced, stable parents with parents at risk for child neglect. Mentors provide support and model positive parenting skills.
- Contact your elected officials and ask them to support funding for programs and policies that support children and families.
- Start or join a community coalition to prevent child abuse and neglect.

Recommended Reading

- *Child Abuse and Neglect: The School's Response,* by Connie Burrows Horton and Tracy K. Cruise (New York: Guilford Press, 2001).
- *A Child Called "It": One Child's Courage to Survive,* by Dave Pelzer (Deerfield Beach, FL: HCI Publishing, 1995).
- *Damaged Parents: An Anatomy of Child Neglect,* edited by Norman A. Polansky (Chicago: University of Chicago Publishing, 1983).

6
SEXUAL ABUSE

Child sexual abuse is sexual activity with a child by an adult, adolescent, or older child. When any adult engages in sexual activity with a child, sexual abuse occurs. Sexual abuse can take on various forms. It can involve sexual intercourse, fondling under or over clothes, or sexual exploitation in which no direct physical action is perpetrated on the child but the child is in the presence of an adult who is clearly becoming sexually aroused by the child's presence. An example of this sexual exploitation is an adult exposing a child to pornography while watching to see what the child does in response. Another example is an adult taking photos of a naked child for personal sexual stimulation. Sexual abuse also includes "exposing private parts to a child or asking the child to expose him or herself, fondling of the genitals or requests for the child to do so, oral sex or attempts to enter the vagina or anus with fingers, objects, or a penis, although actual penetration is rarely achieved" (Coalition for Children, Safe Child Web site). The Internet brings new risks to children. Children can fall victim to cyber sexual predators.

Offenders cross every socioeconomic classification, every race, every sexual orientation, and every educational, ethnic, or cultural description. The most common offender is a married, heterosexual, white male.

Case Study

Fourteen-year-old Daisy is a quiet, soft-spoken, and gregarious girl. She has begun her first year at a new high school and is eager to get to know others in her class. She has been using the computer to connect with friends at her old school and enjoys the chat rooms. She is a likeable girl and seems to get along with everyone. She has begun talking about some unusual contacts she has been having outside the chat rooms. Her new friends are interested in what she has to share, but a few of them have become concerned because she is somewhat secretive about what exactly is going on. When she was at a sleep-over one night, Daisy had unusual nightmares and was not easily consoled. She has also been asking a lot of questions about sexuality that at first seemed age-appropriate but then seemed beyond what her peers were asking. Her eating habits have changed somewhat, and she seems to be losing weight. When asked about what she has been viewing on the computer, she hesitates, gives vague answers, and seems uncomfortable with the question. Daisy alluded to a new friend she met on the Internet. Her friends know the friend is male. What they do not know is that he has been sending pornography to her. He asked to meet her, and she agreed. She was afraid to tell her parents because she knew they would definitely not approve. She did not tell anyone about the encounter and did not dare mention how he had seduced her and convinced her that fondling him and getting her to have sex with him would be a deepening of their relationship. She did not know before she met him that he was not her age, but much older. When she met him, she was too afraid to tell him no and then too ashamed afterward to tell anyone. She knew she should tell. She also knew continuing to meet with him on the Internet was wrong. What she did not know was how to get out of the situation.

Signs and Symptoms

The signs and symptoms of sexual abuse are evident if one knows what to look for. However, the symptoms can be mistaken for other causes and are easily overlooked. One should not assume that if the symptoms are present, sexual abuse has occurred. Yet the signs are important to know so that if symptoms are present, the possibility of sexual abuse can be addressed or at least considered. In any case, whatever is causing the change in behavior needs to be explored further. Youth experiencing sexual abuse may exhibit the following symptoms:

- nightmares, trouble sleeping, or other sleep problems
- spacing out at odd times
- rage, fear, or withdrawal
- sudden mood or behavioral changes either before or after an encounter with an adult
- changes in eating habits (loss of appetite, trouble eating or swallowing)
- unusual fears, such as fear of previously likeable places and people; fear of making friends; fear of situations such as being in the dark or being alone; startled responses to loud noises or voices; and possible paranoia about being watched or chased
- aggressiveness (verbal or physical), defiance, delinquent behavior, excessive risk-taking behaviors
- regression in behavior (i.e., an older child behaving like a younger child by doing such things as wetting the bed or thumb sucking)
- depression, withdrawal, isolation, suicide attempts
- changes in academic performance
- talk about a new older friend
- refusal to talk about a "secret" she or he has with an adult or older child
- reluctance or refusal to be around specific people, such as an uncle or stepparent
- unexplained urinary infections or sexually transmitted diseases
- unexplained bruises, redness, or bleeding from the genitals, anus, or mouth
- frequent headaches, stomachaches, or body aches
- fatigue, tiredness, lack of motivation

- various sexual reactions, from being overly fearful to being promiscuous
- persistent sexual play with other children, themselves, toys, or pets
- displaying sexual knowledge through language or behavior that is beyond what is normal for a child's age
- drug or alcohol problems
- self-mutilating behaviors such as scarring arms with razor blades, needles, or cigarettes

(Adapted from McGlone and Shrader, *Creating Safe and Sacred Places*, pp. 30–31)

Statistics tell us sexual abuse occurs more frequently than we would like to believe. At least one in three to five girls and one in seven to ten boys will be sexually abused at some point in their childhood ("Stop It Now!" The Campaign to Prevent Child Sexual Abuse Web site). Every two minutes a child is sexually assaulted, and 50–90 percent of child sexual assaults are never reported. Often there are *no* physical signs (Love Our Children USA Web site).

Children often will not tell adults about the abuse they have experienced, because they are afraid they will not be believed, or the perpetrator has threatened them or their family with harm if they do tell. In addition, abuse victims often feel ashamed and responsible for the abuse. Sexually abused boys tend to report the abuse less often than sexually abused girls. Most of the time, the offender is known to the child or the child's family. Often the abuser is a family member.

Response, Diagnosis, and Treatment

When a youth makes any comment about the possibility of sexual abuse, it is critical she be believed and taken seriously. *It is rare for children to lie about abuse.* Refrain from making any judgmental comments, and allow the young person to talk freely. Assure the child she did the right thing by telling. Let the child know she is not responsible for the abuse and not to blame for it as well. Tell the young person you will take appropriate steps to do what you can to stop the abuse. It is important to tell the child you cannot keep her secret and you must report the abuse. *Never* promise a young person you will not tell her secret. Each state identifies mandatory reporters (groups of people who are required to report suspicions of child abuse). However, any concerned person can and should report suspected child abuse. A report is not an accusation; it is an expression of concern and a request for an investigation or evaluation of the child's situation.

Any suspicion of sexual abuse *must* to be reported. This includes suspicion of cyber sexual abuse. You do not have to verify the abuse; you only need to report it. People who report suspected abuse in good faith cannot be prosecuted. To report suspicion of abuse, contact your local child protection agency.

Once a report is made, the receiving agency will determine the extent of the abuse. The abuser will be contacted, and more important, the child or children will be given safety. Whether the abuse is substantiated or unsubstantiated, services are available to the family to help them through the crisis of a report having been made and information found that would warrant such services. These services could include in-home family therapy, a safety plan for the family, individual therapy for the child, and further investigation of the circumstances surrounding the report.

Pastoral Care Strategies

An adult working with a youth who has been sexually abused or is suspected of being abused needs to be supportive and caring. This is the first step in helping the child and re-establishing the trust that was lost by the abuse. Watch your reaction. How you react will determine how the child feels about himself and the abuse. Be careful not to overreact or underreact. Other strategies to keep in mind:

- Do not assume anything about anyone.
- Respond promptly to all allegations of abuse.
- Reach out to all victims and their families and communicate sincere commitment to their spiritual and emotional well-being.
- Be a safe, responsible, and consistent resource person for the youth.

- Set clear boundaries with all young people; that is, do not intrude beyond their comfort zone either verbally or physically.
- Know your local resources and how to use them, such as therapists who offer counseling with children and adolescent victims of sexual abuse.
- Ensure your parish has a written statement clearly indicating conduct considered unacceptable, unethical, and illegal by the community, the diocese, the Church, and county and state civil authorities. Provide a copy of this statement to all adults who have direct contact with young people.
- Develop clearly determined procedures for community members to file complaints (including the designation of a specific person within the community to whom a complaint can be made). Be certain this procedure is posted in visible locations throughout your facilities.
- Learn who to call to make a report of abuse.
- Know the difference between appropriate sexual behavior and behavior that would indicate abuse may have occurred.
- Offer to take young people who have been abused to support groups available in the area.
- Make space available in local churches or schools for support groups for sexually abused youth.
- Provide youth and families with abuse prevention programming and training.
- Include annual prayer services and masses of healing for abuse victims.

Recommended Reading

- *Creating Safe and Sacred Places: Identifying, Preventing, and Healing Sexual Abuse,* by Gerard J. McGlone and Mary Shrader with Laurie Delgatto (Winona, MN: Saint Mary's Press, 2003).
- *How Long Does It Hurt? A Guide to Recovering from Incest and Sexual Abuse for Teenagers, Their Friends, and Their Families,* by Cynthia Mather (San Francisco: Jossey-Bass, 1994).
- *Invisible Girls: The Truth About Sexual Abuse — A Book for Teen Girls, Young Women, and Everyone Who Cares About Them,* by Patti

Feuereisen and Caroline Pincus (Emeryville, CA: Seal Press, 2005).

- *When Your Child Has Been Molested: A Parent's Guide to Healing and Recovery,* by Kathryn Brohl and Joyce Case Potter (San Francisco: Jossey-Bass, 2004).

7

EMOTIONAL AND PHYSICAL ABUSE

Although emotional and physical abuse may seem to be two very different types of abuse, they have many common characteristics and long-term, negative effects. Both involve violence to the well-being of the victim. Each is among the most common forms of abuse experienced by youth. Though physical abuse is more obvious externally, emotional abuse can be observed by its effects. Emotional abuse is defined as "the systematic tearing down of another human being. It is considered a pattern of behavior that can seriously interfere with a child's positive development" (National Exchange Club Foundation Web site).

Emotional abuse can involve a variety of behaviors that might include frequent criticizing, belittling, insulting, rejecting, teasing, ignoring, terrorizing, or corrupting (witnessing or participating in drug or alcohol use, cruel behavior to people or animals, or criminal activities). No matter what the behavior is, the youth is affected negatively.

Physical abuse, on the other hand, is defined as "any act which results in a non-accidental trauma or physical injury. Inflicted physical injury most often represents unreasonable, severe corporal punishment or unjustifiable punishment. Physical abuse injuries result from punching, beating, kicking, biting, burning, or otherwise harming a child" (National Exchange Club Foundation Web site).

Case Study

Lately Stuart seemed unusually quiet and withdrawn. He also had some bruises he attempted to cover up either by wearing long sleeves in warm weather or by stating he "fell again" or "ran into something." At the times when he was most quiet, he seemed reluctant to go home and overly compliant to requests from adults around him. Everyone knew he did not have any other family in the area and his parents were having financial problems. His dad had been out of work for a while, and his mother was having difficulty getting a job that paid more than minimum wage. When his dad came to pick Stuart up, he frequently called Stuart names such as "loser," "worthless," "no good," or "never going to amount to anything." Stuart often looked uncomfortable around his dad and appeared to want to avoid him as much as possible.

Signs and Symptoms

Even though emotional abuse may not leave marks like physical abuse, both may be difficult to detect because youth tend to cover up the signs. Youth suffering from physical or emotional abuse may exhibit the following symptoms:
- shyness, passivity, compliance
- aggressiveness
- obvious anxiety and fears
- anger and rage
- self-destructive or self-abusive behaviors
- inability to trust others
- school problems or failures
- clinginess or withdrawal
- sadness or depression
- refusal to undress for gym class

- inconsistent reasons for injuries
- fear of parents
- difficulty getting along with others
- complaints of pain with movement or contact
- history of running away from home
- insecurity and poor self-esteem
- alcohol or drug abuse
- difficulty forming relationships
- flashbacks
- nightmares or other sleep problems

Physical abuse accounts for the majority of reports of abuse. Reasons for abuse vary. Sometimes parents are unable to cope with their life situation and take it out on their children. Sometimes parents have been abused themselves and have not had good role models for appropriate parenting. Sometimes parents have problems with alcohol and are abusive when they are drinking. Other times parents have not gotten their own needs met and do not have the wherewithal to handle the stresses of parenting.

Often children will not tell anyone about the abuse, and it will not be discovered until adolescence or adulthood, when relationships are affected or abusive actions are noticed with peers or in dating situations.

Response, Diagnosis, and Treatment

As with other forms of abuse, when there is suspicion of emotional or physical abuse, it is imperative to report it to the local child protective services agency. The longer the abuse continues, the more difficult it is to treat, and the more damage is done to the victim. Child protective services will determine if abuse has occurred and what services are recommended for the child and his family. Sometimes the suspicion is minimal but there is a feeling that something is not right. It is important, again, to make a report because a particular incident may be part of a number of incidents reported by others and will confirm more firmly that abuse has been occurring. Sometimes youth will ask that you not tell anyone when abuse is noticed. When that is requested, you must tell the young person you cannot promise not to tell if he is in danger of being hurt. It is against the law for you not to tell. You can assure the youth that you will keep him as safe as possible, but you will have to tell someone who will help him get to a safe place.

When emotional or physical abuse is reported, child protective services interviews the parties involved separately. Often the youth will be interviewed before the parents know about the report to reduce the threat of harm to the child. Often the young person will be interviewed in a familiar place, such as the school, to allow him to feel safe and unintimidated.

Depending on the extent of the abuse, the young person may be allowed to go home while family support services are being arranged. However, when the abuse is extensive, often the perpetrator will be required to leave the home, or if that is not possible, the child will be put in foster care. In cases of emotional abuse, education about appropriate parenting and family support is the first step of action for remedying the situation. With physical abuse, an assessment of the potential for harm to the child is made, and action is taken based on the results of that assessment. Often physical abuse is paired with emotional abuse, and the two are treated simultaneously. In treatment, generally the child is seen individually to assess the effects of the abuse on him. He might also be seen with the nonoffending parent in order to garner support for the child. Therapy might also consist of the youth talking about his feelings regarding the abuse, especially anger, betrayal, fear, and confusion. The youth would be encouraged to look at his strengths and see how he has been able to survive to this point. An emphasis in therapy would be to help the youth understand the abuse was definitely not his fault, and he had no responsibility for the choices made by the adults in his life. Therapy would end with the youth being able to acknowledge his worth, have goals for the future, and be able to trust that there are caring adults in his life who will not harm him.

Pastoral Care Strategies

Adults who work with youth need to be aware of the potential for abuse. It is naïve to think that abuse does not happen to children in any particular area, any particular socioeconomic group, or with any specific religious affiliation. In your own ministry to and with young people, keep these strategies in mind:

• Believe the young person who says he is being abused.

• Advocate for a parenting group in your community.

• Offer training for adults who work with youth to identify and recognize abuse of children and teens.

• Offer opportunities for parents in the neighborhood to get to know one another and develop mutual support systems.

• Find ways for parents to get support on parenting issues when they need it. Possibilities include classes, support groups, tip sheets in bulletins and newsletters, and resource libraries.

• Respond to family crises. Offer extra support to families when they need it, as in times of illness, job loss, housing problems, and other stressors.

• Link families to services and opportunities. Provide referrals for job training, education, health care, mental health, and other essential services in the community.

• Discuss abuse issues with other adults in order to better recognize when it is present.

• Provide support groups for children and adolescents who are being or have been abused.

• Facilitate children's social and emotional development. Some programs use curriculums that focus specifically on helping children articulate their feelings and get along with others. When children bring home what they learn in the classroom, parents benefit as well.

Recommended Reading

- *Emotional Abuse: The Trauma and the Treatment,* by Marti Tamm Loring (San Francisco: Jossey-Bass, 1998).
- *My Father's Child: Help and Healing for the Victims of Emotional, Sexual, and Physical Abuse,* by Lynda D. Elliott and Vicki L. Tanner (Brentwood, TN: Wolgemuth and Hyatt Publishers, 1988).
- *You Don't Know Me,* by David Klass (New York: HarperTempest, 2002).

8
DATING VIOLENCE

Dating violence is a pattern of violent behavior for the purpose of maintaining control over the other person. It can be physical, emotional, verbal, or sexual. It is found across all socioeconomic, racial, ethnic, and religious groups. Dating violence is not about an occasional disagreement or conflict. Rather, it is about fear and intimidation. It can manifest itself in extreme possessiveness; verbal put-downs; forced intimacy; isolation from friends and family; hitting, pushing, punching, biting, scratching; or even statements of harm to self if the partner does not comply with requests. Although both boys and girls can be violent toward each other, there are some differences between them. Girls tend to yell, pinch, slap, kick, scratch, or threaten self-harm. Boys cause more physical harm and are more likely to punch or force their partner into sexual activity.

Teens are especially vulnerable to dating violence because of their inexperience with dating; often they are still discovering what a healthy relationship looks like. Dating violence may appear "romantic" to teens because their partner seems to care about them enough to "fight" for them, but there is nothing romantic about this kind of abuse.

Case Study

Trish had just turned sixteen, and her parents allowed her to date for the first time. Jared was the boy of her dreams. She had known him throughout middle school, and now they were both juniors in high school. They had dated only a few times, but she knew he was "the one." He wanted to be with her all the time. He called her frequently during the day and wanted to know where she was when they were not together. It seemed so romantic to her. No one had ever paid that kind of attention to her. It bothered her to give up her girlfriends, but this relationship was so much more exciting. Jared meant so much more than anyone ever had. At first she thought the names he called her when she made mistakes were a little upsetting, but eventually she got used to them and thought they were okay. Nothing could ruin their relationship, and she wasn't going to let something like name-calling get in the way.

The day Jared pushed her when he was upset was a bit disconcerting, but he apologized and said he didn't know what was wrong with him, but it certainly wouldn't happen again. Trish was so happy; she was not going to let an accident get in the way of their being together. The second time Jared pushed her was again disturbing, but his apologies were so sincere that Trish believed he really meant it when he said it would not happen again. But the night he became physically abusive to her when they were making out after a movie was extremely upsetting. He did not want to accept her "no" when he wanted more than kissing and a little petting. This time she was scared. She was not ready for more intimacy, but he seemed to want more. She thought she would lose him if she said no, and then the extreme pushing, shoving, and bruising she experienced totally confused her.

Maybe Jared wasn't perfect. Maybe she was giving up too much to be with him. But he said such nice things, he seemed to want to be with her, and he was so contrite after an argument. She thought he was in love with her. She did not spend time with her friends, she was afraid of getting on Jared's "bad side," she felt responsible for his pushing and hitting her, she did not feel good about herself anymore, and she was unsure where she was heading.

Signs and Symptoms

Vulnerability to dating violence is high among teens, especially those least experienced in dating. They may be unaware of the violence until it becomes extreme. It is helpful for adults to be attuned to changes in teens' attitudes and behaviors so concerns can be expressed and guidance or outside help can be given or recommended. Victims of dating violence may exhibit the following symptoms:

- new eating or sleeping patterns
- anger
- poor school performance
- skipping school or being afraid of going to school
- hopelessness and helplessness
- headaches or stomachaches
- difficulty concentrating
- clinginess to their dating partner
- depression
- drug or alcohol use
- nightmares or other sleep disturbances
- anxiety
- withdrawal from peer relationships
- unexplainable bruises, scratches, and injuries

One in three teenagers has experienced violence in a dating relationship (The National Center for Victims of Crime, "Teen Dating Violence" fact sheet). Yet teenagers tend to think they are the only ones experiencing any kind of dating violence. The use of alcohol or drugs increases the likelihood of violence. Alcohol and drugs are also used to dull the pain of the experience of violence. When violence occurs, adolescents are often ashamed, confused, and even in denial that a problem exists. Sometimes teens will confide in their friends but are afraid to tell adults because of shame, worry they may not be believed, fear of being punished themselves, or fear of retaliation by the abuser.

Response, Diagnosis, and Treatment

Youth who are beginning a dating relationship are often so enthralled with having a relationship they do not see the potential dangers of a relationship going awry. They can be in denial for long periods of time, which often creates greater problems with serious, long-term consequences.

If no crime has been committed but the victim is experiencing emotional difficulties, listening in a nonjudgmental manner, being supportive, and not blaming the victim are primary. From there it is important to let the victim's parents know of your concern. Sometimes young people do not want anyone to know they are having difficulties; they claim their parents either don't care or would not understand. Regardless, you should be in contact with the parents. Strongly encourage professional counseling to help the young person understand the consequences of violence in relationships and as a means of support as she considers ending the relationship.

If a crime such as physical or sexual assault has been committed, it is mandatory that it be reported to the police. Sometimes the teen may request that no report be made because of the consequences for the abuser and for the victim. Explaining to the victim the necessity of making the report to prevent future violence is important. Explain that mandatory reporting is also required of you.

If the young person is fearful of further harm (emotional, sexual, or physical), a restraining order to prevent further contact is an option. A restraining order or an order for protection is a court order requiring that contact between two parties does not occur. A restraining order is not a guarantee of safety because it can be broken, but it is the beginning of a legal process that makes the abuser aware of the seriousness of the situation. An adult usually has to ask for the order on behalf of a minor. Parents with the assistance of a trained counselor (and possibly a legal representative) should request such an order. Each state has varying rules for a minor to obtain an order for protection. A good way to start the process is to contact a local social service agency in the area or the local police department.

When physical safety is at risk, it is imperative to make a safety plan for the teen. This can include having numbers of contact people available, such as the police, friends, and trusted adults; community resources, such as women's resources or shelters; and alternative transportation, such as a taxi. Having a buddy system for going to and from school, knowing how to get away from a dangerous situation, and being informed of where to go for help are also useful strategies for keeping a young person safe.

Treatment for victims of dating violence begins when the victim is willing to admit some sort of violence has occurred. Talking about the violence is a first step. Sharing the feelings associated with the violence is a second step. Being able to acknowledge that feelings are involved and naming them helps the healing process begin. A person trained to work with victims of violence will be able to help the victim disclose the necessary information, make a safety plan, report the violence to the appropriate authorities, obtain an order for protection (if necessary), and empower the individual to regain control of her life.

Pastoral Care Strategies

An adult working with a youth who has been personally violated in a relationship needs to keep in mind that no matter how minor the incident seems to the adult, if the youth is not able to function like he did before the incident, it is a serious matter and needs to be treated as such. Sensitivity to the other person's perceptions and feelings is of utmost importance. The adult must also be careful not to overreact, because the young person will be looking to the adult for guidance on how to handle the situation. In your own ministry to and with young people, keep these strategies in mind:

- Become educated about healthy relationships as well as dating violence.
- Report criminal behavior to the appropriate authorities.
- Learn about area resources of support for victims.
- Foster discussion and education on healthy relationships.

- Remind young people they always have the right to say no.
- Talk to young people about love. Tell them jealousy is not a sign of love. Possessiveness is not a sign of love. Respect is the sign they are looking for in a partner.
- Start a peer education program on teen dating violence.
- Ask your school library to purchase books about living without violence and the cycle of domestic violence.
- Create bulletin boards in church and school classrooms to raise awareness of dating violence.

Recommended Reading

- *Dangerous Dating: Helping Young Women Say No to Abusive Relationships,* by Patricia Riddle Gaddis (Dallas: Shaw Publishing, 2000).
- *Dating Violence: Young Women in Danger,* by Barrie Levy (Emeryville, CA: Seal Press, 1998).
- *Ending Violence in Teen Dating Relationships: A Resource Guide for Parents and Pastors,* by Al Miles (Minneapolis: Augsburg Press, 2005).

9
GANG INVOLVEMENT

Gangs have been around for many years but recently have changed in their composition. They used to be limited primarily to young males of minority groups. They were in low socioeconomic neighborhoods and typically did not involve people from religious groups. However, as more young people have more time on their hands, less supervision, and more money, the makeup of gangs has changed. What has not changed is the focus of gang behavior. Most commonly the word *gang* refers to street gangs: groups who take over territory ("turf") in a particular city. A youth gang is commonly thought of as a self-formed association of peers having the following characteristics: a gang name and recognizable symbols, identifiable leadership, a geographic territory, a regular meeting pattern, and collective actions to carry out illegal activities.

Gangs often use intimidation and fear to maintain control of their territory or group. They have a pattern of violent behavior — including physical, emotional, verbal, and sexual violence — to identify themselves. Gang members come from a variety of socioeconomic backgrounds; they are found in urban and rural settings; they include members of both genders, all races, and all ethnic and religious makeups. Teens join gangs for a variety of reasons. Some are seeking excitement; others are looking for prestige, protection, a chance to make money, or a sense of belonging.

Case Study

Travis is a twelve-year-old boy who has two older brothers. His brothers are involved in after-school athletic programs and have little time to spend with Travis. He is not interested in sports and does not have any particular hobby or interest. He enjoys being around others but feels somewhat alienated from his family. Recently his parents have noticed he is more secretive than usual. He has been caught smoking cigarettes a couple times, and his parents have noticed that some of their alcoholic beverage supply has been tampered with. They think this is a stage Travis is going through and have generally ignored it except to tell him they do not approve. His friends have noticed he has withdrawn from them and has begun hanging out with kids their parents do not approve of. They have encouraged Travis to do things with them, but he seems more interested in these other kids who are known gang members. Travis's brothers have noticed that he has been wearing the same color clothes repeatedly. On one occasion, his dad saw some strange symbols on his math notebook cover but again thought it was an interesting symbol and ignored it as a preteen phase.

The police came to Travis's parents' house one evening wondering if they knew anything about Travis being involved in spraying some graffiti on a business downtown. His parents denied any knowledge of his involvement, but when asked where he was and who he was with that particular night, they admitted they had been trusting he was with his friends who, according to Travis, were going to a movie. What they found out was that Travis had been lying to them about his friends. He was not with his old friends, but with new friends who were gang members. He had been smoking and drinking and experimenting a little with marijuana, and he had begun other risky behaviors, such as shoplifting spray paint and painting graffiti in order to fit in with these friends.

Signs and Symptoms

Kids at risk of involvement with gangs are those who are marginalized — that is, they do not feel they fit in with their family or friends. They are willing to do things outside their "comfort zone" to belong and be accepted. Kids who have unsupervised time, have few limits set on them, and are not held accountable for their activities are at greatest risk. Gang members often are not socially adept, have low self-esteem, have poor problem-solving abilities, have a tendency to be impulsive, have poor communication skills, are attracted to risky or delinquent behaviors, and are not attached to people in general. The following signs and symptoms are indicative of possible gang involvement:

- rule breaking on a regular basis
- staying out late with no good reason
- withdrawal from family and former friends
- unusual desire for secrecy
- signs of drug use
- gang-style slang
- trouble with the police
- unusual interest in gangster-influenced music, videos, movies, or Web sites
- specific drawings or gang symbols on schoolbooks, clothes, walls, or tattoos
- unexplained cash or material possessions, such as clothing or jewelry
- unusual interest in one or two particular colors of clothing or a particular logo
- weapon(s)
- decreasing performance at school
- change in attitude about school, church, or other normal activities

- phone threats to the family from unknown callers
- discipline problems at school, church, or other activities
- use of a new nickname
- physical signs of having been in a fight

Gang involvement can begin as early as elementary school. Children as young as seven to eight years old have been recruited to work for gangs. Once in the gang, the child's behavior may change either suddenly or gradually, but it will follow a pattern. To be accepted by the gang, he must adopt a defiant attitude toward authority figures. This defiance may be expressed by violent behavior at school or home. When at home, the new gang member's defiance may or may not manifest itself in violence, depending on the relationship with his parents and other family members. However, if the family interferes with the child's gang involvement, there may be repeated confrontations.

Response, Diagnosis, and Treatment

Youth who fall prey to gang seduction pay a high price for membership. Initiation rights often involve committing serious and sometimes violent crimes. Gang membership almost guarantees one a criminal record, not to mention the physical risks and dangers of violent activities. The physical risks and dangers apply not only to the gang member but to family members and innocent bystanders as well.

It is critical at young ages for children to know gang involvement is not a good choice. By letting them know of adult disapproval and of serious legal consequences, they may think over involvement before they decide to experiment.

If you suspect a young person is interested or involved in gang activity, your first response should be to inform the youth's parents. If criminal activity is involved or has been alleged, you must also contact the proper authorities.

Proper treatment for a young person involved in gang activity will vary depending on the depth of the involvement. If there has been criminal activity, the youth may be charged with a criminal offense and may have to appear in court. If the youth has a relatively clean record and healthy support systems, he may be sentenced to community service, be placed on probation, and not be allowed contact with any gang members. He may be fined for damage of property and may be ordered by the court to receive counseling on problem solving, avoiding peer pressure, and understanding the connection between choices and consequences. If the crime committed is serious, the young person may be sent to a juvenile detention facility. Parents may be ordered to attend parenting skills training, and the family may be required to attend family therapy to improve their communication skills and repair the damage caused by the youth's behaviors. Sometimes a physical move may be necessary to get out of the gang's territory so the youth is not pressured or threatened to return.

When no criminal behavior has occurred or the youth has not been caught in criminal behavior, he should be encouraged to seek counseling for reasons previously mentioned as well as to determine the underlying causes for his attraction to the gang.

Pastoral Care Strategies

Adults working with young people who are or have been involved with gangs need to recognize young people's need to be accepted and included. Providing unconditional acceptance of youth is critical. Letting them know they are cared about and that there is genuine concern for their welfare is important. Support for the difficulty they are experiencing or feeling will go a long way to engaging them. Agreeing with or accepting the behavior or attitude is not helpful. Being a role model for healthy choices under difficult circumstances is a good beginning.

In your own ministry to and with young people, keep these strategies in mind:
- Discourage youth from hanging around with gangs.
- Cooperate with authorities when youth are involved with gangs.
- Occupy young peoples' free time with positive activities.
- Teach respect for others' property.

- When gang symbols or graffiti is found on youths' possessions, confront the behavior and do not allow such symbols or graffiti to be visible.
- Do not allow gang-related clothing in public.
- Support neighborhood watch groups, or begin one if there is none present.
- Plan activities at times when youth would otherwise be unsupervised, such as after school or on nonschool days.
- Conduct discussions on gang-related topics, such as the need to fit in, peer pressure, and consequences of criminal behavior.
- Find out about gang activity in your community. Learn about gangs, gang recruitment, activities, signs, and colors. Then share the information by publishing an article in a school or local newspaper, or by talking to community groups, parents, or groups of students.
- Join an existing group working to get rid of gangs in your school or community, or launch your own effort.
- Invite a former gang member or gang expert to speak to youth and parents.
- Contact local law enforcement officials to find out more about gang prevention programs in your area. Invite representatives from a prevention program to speak to youth.
- Challenge young people and adult leaders to explore ways your church or community can be a place that teaches a sense of belonging that dispels the attractiveness of gangs.

Recommended Reading

- *Always Running: La Vida Loco: Gang Days in L.A.,* by Luis J. Rodriguez (New York: Touchstone Publishers, 2005).
- *Gangs, Graffiti, and Violence: A Realistic Guide to the Scope and Nature of Gangs in America,* by Duane A. Leet, George E. Rush, and Anthony M. Smith (Stamford, CT: Wadsworth Publishing, 2000).
- *Life in the Gang: Family, Friends, and Violence,* by Scott H. Decker, Barrik van Winkle, and Alfred Blumstein (Cambridge, England: Cambridge University Press, 1996).

SECTION THREE
DISORDERS

Whereas the previous chapters addressed issues found in *some* of the population, many of the following disorders are much more typically found in the general population. Some are talked about openly, such as depression and anxiety; others have more of a stigma, such as schizophrenia and explosive disorders. All these disorders affect everyday functioning, get in the way of healthy relationships, and can prevent a young person from living a full and healthy life.

10
EATING DISORDERS

Eating disorders such as anorexia, bulimia, and compulsive eating include extreme emotions, attitudes, and behaviors surrounding weight and food issues. They are serious emotional and physical problems that can have life-threatening consequences for both females and males.

Anorexia Nervosa

This disorder is the most deadly of the eating disorders. It involves malnutrition and refusal to gain weight. The person with anorexia nervosa does not see herself as she actually is, but rather perceives herself as fat and tries to become thinner and thinner. She may use laxatives, enemas, or diuretics as well as vomiting to rid herself of any food she eats. She may increase her exercise to lose weight as well. Anorexia isn't just a problem with food or weight. It's an attempt to use food and weight to deal with emotional problems.

Case Study

Mandy is a sixteen-year-old girl who has been extremely active and athletic. She was worried about how she was going to pay for college and decided getting a part-time job after school would ease her worries and help her out financially. Her work was pretty sedentary—serving refreshments or taking tickets at the local movie theater. Because she was working after school, she had to give up her extracurricular involvement at school, including athletics. She was an A student and was conscientious about doing whatever she did extremely well.

Soon Mandy began to notice she was not only gaining weight, but fat was appearing around her thighs, hips, and stomach. She wasn't sure what she could do about it but decided that cutting down on what she was eating would be a first step. That worked some, but she was not satisfied with the results. She began weighing herself daily, but the weight was not coming off as rapidly as she would like. Her next plan was to exercise by getting up early in the morning and running. She began to increase her running by rising a little earlier every morning. This too was somewhat effective, but she was still not feeling good about how she looked. Using laxatives would get the weight off faster, so that was her next plan. She began staying up late to do exercises in her bedroom, getting up early in the morning to run, decreasing her food intake, counting every calorie that went into her body, weighing herself sometimes two and three times a day. Friends would comment that she was looking too thin, but she began to believe there was no such thing as "too thin."

Signs and Symptoms

Anorexia nervosa often begins slowly. It becomes noticeable when a young person starts showing considerable weight loss without an awareness of the loss. Often the youth will comment that she wants to lose more weight even when others think she is getting too thin.

The disorder begins to take on a life of its own and at that point is difficult to change. A young person battling anorexia nervosa may display the following symptoms:

- refusal to maintain body weight at or above a minimally normal weight for age and height
- constant exercising
- intense fear of gaining weight or becoming fat, despite being underweight or losing a significant amount of weight
- frequent weighing or talking about weight
- skipping meals frequently or counting every calorie when choosing foods
- depressed mood, social withdrawal
- irritability
- insomnia
- self-induced vomiting or abuse of laxatives, diuretics, or enemas
- preoccupation with thoughts of food
- perfectionism
- concerns about eating in public
- intolerance to cold
- development of lanugo — fine, downy hair on body trunk
- yellowing of skin
- dental enamel erosion and calluses on the back of the hand from contact with teeth while inducing vomiting

Anorexia is significantly more common among girls than boys. It usually begins in middle to late adolescence. It is not true that anorexics are never hungry. They are always hungry. Feeling hunger gives them a feeling of control over their lives and their bodies. It makes them feel like they are good at something — they are good at losing weight.

Response, Diagnosis, and Treatment

Anyone who suffers from this disorder requires professional help. If you are concerned that a young person might be anorexic, let her parents know of your concern and perhaps plan with them a strategy to intervene. Contact a professional to facilitate these efforts. Generally an observation of physical symptoms and a personal history will quickly confirm the diagnosis of anorexia.

Treatment of anorexia is difficult because people with anorexia often believe there is nothing wrong with them. Patients in the early stages of anorexia (less than six months or with just a small amount of weight loss) may be successfully treated without having to be admitted to the hospital. But for successful treatment, patients must want to change and must have family and friends to help them.

People with more serious anorexia need care in the hospital, usually in a special unit for people with eating disorders. Treatment consisting of therapy with a team of professionals is the most successful. The team often includes a nutritionist, a physician, and a therapist skilled in eating disorders. Treatment involves more than changing the person's eating habits. Anorexic patients often need counseling so they can work on changing the feelings causing their eating problems. These feelings may be about their weight, their family problems, or their self-esteem.

Bulimia

Bulimia differs from anorexia in that the person's weight is near normal or slightly above average. The person with bulimia is aware that her eating is not normal and is afraid she will not be able to stop eating. Bulimia is characterized by episodes of binge eating followed by inappropriate methods of weight control (purging). Inappropriate methods of weight control include vomiting, fasting, enemas, excessive use of laxatives and diuretics, or compulsive exercising. Excessive shape and weight concerns are also characteristics of bulimia.

A binge is an episode where an individual eats a much larger amount of food than most people would in a similar situation. Binge eating is not a response to intense hunger. It is usually a response to depression, stress, or self-esteem issues. During the binge episode, the individual experiences a loss of control. However, the sense of a loss of control is also followed by a short-lived calmness. The calmness is often followed by self-loathing. The cycle of overeating and purging usually becomes an obsession and is repeated often.

Case Study

Jenny is a junior in high school. She has always had some problems with her weight. She has tried diets without success. She is getting ready for prom and wants to lose some weight in the next month. She thought she might starve herself for a couple days but finds that after fasting, she makes up for the lost time by eating large amounts of food. So she figures all she has to do is vomit after eating. No one notices she has increased her caloric intake, because she doesn't tell anyone she has found out she can eat to her heart's delight, throw up, and continue on as though she hadn't eaten so much. She is not losing weight, but she is not gaining weight either. The problem is she doesn't feel good about herself; she feels out of control and is beginning to throw up without giving it much thought. Her friends and family are noticing she is withdrawing and seems much more irritable. Her parents are noticing Jenny will go to the bathroom after eating a normal meal with the family.

Signs and Symptoms

Bulimia also begins in subtle ways that can easily go unnoticed. Keeping an eye out for unusual behaviors around eating is helpful in detecting the beginnings of this dangerous disorder. Young people with bulimia may display the following characteristics:

- secretive eating
- frequent trips to the bathroom after eating
- unexplained disappearance of food in large amounts
- depression, irritability
- drug and alcohol use in addition to eating difficulties
- dental problems involving loss of tooth enamel
- eating an inordinate amount of food in a short time period, for example, two hours or less
- abuse of laxatives, diuretics, or enemas
- vomiting easily on demand
- excessive exercising

There is currently no definite known cause of bulimia. Researchers believe it begins with dissatisfaction with the person's body and extreme concern with body size and shape. Usually individuals suffering from bulimia have low self-esteem, feelings of helplessness, and a fear of becoming fat.

Response, Diagnosis, and Treatment

As with anorexia, denial and secrecy complicate the diagnosis of bulimia. Truthful disclosure of behaviors is critical for an accurate diagnosis. Anyone who suffers from this disorder requires professional help. If you are concerned a young person might be bulimic, let her parents know of your concern and perhaps plan with them a strategy to intervene. Contact a professional to facilitate these efforts.

Some people who suffer from bulimia may require hospitalization owing to the extent of the medical or psychological complications. Others may require outpatient programs. Still others may require only weekly counseling and monitoring by a therapist or physician. The primary goals of treatment should address both the physical and the psychological needs of the young person to restore physical health and normal eating patterns. The young person needs to identify internal feelings and distorted beliefs that led to the disorder initially. An appropriate treatment approach addresses underlying issues of control, self-perception, and family dynamics. Nutritional education and behavior management provide healthy alternatives to weight management. Group counseling or support groups can assist in the recovery process as well.

Compulsive Overeating

People suffering with compulsive overeating (also known as "binge eating") have what is characterized as an addiction to food; they use food and eating as a way to hide from their emotions, to fill a void they feel inside, and to cope with daily stresses and problems in their lives. People with this disorder tend to be overweight and are usually aware their eating habits are abnormal, but they find little comfort because of society's tendency to stereotype the overweight individual. Comments like "just go on a diet" are as emotionally devastating to a person suffering from compulsive overeating as "just eat" can be to a person dealing with anorexia.

Compulsive overeating is characterized primarily by periods of uncontrolled, impulsive, or continuous eating beyond the point of feeling comfortably full. Although there is no purging, there may be sporadic fasts or repetitive diets and often feelings of shame or self-hatred after a binge.

Case Study

Billy comes from a family of overweight people. He has been teased since he was six years old, and now that he is sixteen, he has given up on being accepted by his peers. He likes to eat and especially likes burgers from fast-food restaurants. Now that he has a job, he can pretty much eat what he wants between meals. And his mother is a good cook, so he eats well at home too. His favorite pastime is sitting in front of the TV with a bowl of potato chips and a can or two of soda. What else is he supposed to do? Interact with his peers? That would just involve more teasing. He is painfully aware of the problems of being overweight. Billy often feels guilty for not being "good enough"; he is ashamed of being overweight, and he has low self-esteem. He knows he uses food and eating to cope with these feelings. Billy turns to obsessive episodes of binging and eating as a way to forget the pain he feels and the desire for affection he needs.

Signs and Symptoms

It is easy to see when someone is grossly overweight. However, it is insidious and difficult to change. Young people suffering with compulsive overeating may have these symptoms:

- fear of not being able to control eating
- fear of eating around and with others
- chronic dieting on a variety of popular diet plans
- holding the belief that life will be better if he can lose weight
- hiding food in strange places (closets, cabinets, suitcases, under the bed) to eat at a later time
- vague or secretive eating patterns
- self-defeating statements after food consumption
- blaming failure in the social or professional community on weight
- believing food is his only friend
- frequently out of breath after relatively light activities
- excessive sweating and shortness of breath
- decreased mobility due to weight gain
- mood swings, depression, fatigue
- insomnia, poor sleeping habits

Because binge eating often centers around consuming foods high in fat and sugar, many sufferers may not be getting the nutrients they need. The depression often associated with the disorder is a constant health difficulty. The obesity that regularly arises from the disorder can also lead to diabetes, high blood pressure, high cholesterol, and a variety of other health conditions.

Response, Diagnosis, and Treatment

Many young people with eating disorders have trouble admitting they have a problem and may not want to seek treatment. Having trusted people around them can help encourage them to get the help they need. If you think a young person may be suffering from compulsive overeating disorder, speak with his parent and encourage professional counseling as quickly as possible. If untreated, compulsive overeating will become part of a destructive cycle that can continue for years and cause significant health problems for the young person.

Several options are available for people who want help controlling this disorder. Cognitive behavior therapy (CBT) teaches people how to keep track of their eating, how to change their unhealthy eating habits, and how to modify the way they react in difficult situations. Interpersonal psychotherapy helps people look at their relationships with friends and family and make changes in problem areas. Drug therapy, such as antidepressants, may be helpful for some people. Paired with the therapy and drug options, a weight-loss program can also be helpful.

Pastoral Care Strategies

Most of us want to have healthy, well-functioning, and attractive bodies. However, our celebrity-smitten society places undue emphasis on the attractiveness part, and then tells us that to be attractive, we must be thin. Our normal desire to maintain a healthy body weight can become abnormal when we are constantly under peer and societal pressure to attain and maintain a weight and shape that is not natural for us. In your own ministry to and with young people, keep these strategies in mind:

- Be aware of the signs and symptoms of eating disorders.
- Know of resources in the area for referral for professional help and for support groups.
- Accept young people for who they are and recognize their positive qualities beyond their weight or body shape.
- Be a positive role model for healthy eating.
- Create bulletin boards showing healthy eating strategies along with the new food pyramid.
- Invite speakers who are knowledgeable about eating disorders and how to prevent them or deal with them to speak to young people and parents.
- Serve only healthy and nutritional snacks and meals at meetings and events.
- Offer alternative physical activities for youth who may be handicapped by weight and unable to keep up with their peers.
- Engage young people in conversations about healthy body image.
- Invite a nutritionist to come speak to parents of younger children on developing healthy eating patterns in children.

- Teach young people to eat for the right reasons. Invite conversation about the concept of emotional eating.
- Help young people to effectively deconstruct media messages regarding weight and body image.

Recommended Reading

- *Help Your Teenager Beat an Eating Disorder,* by James Lock and Daniel le Grange (New York: The Guilford Press, 2005).
- *Insatiable — The Compelling Story of Four Teens, Food, and Its Power,* by Eve Eliot (Deerfield Beach, FL: HCI Teens, 2001).
- *Talking to Eating Disorders: Simple Ways to Support Someone with Anorexia, Bulimia, Binge Eating, or Body Image Issues,* by Jeanne Albronda Heaton and Claudia J. Strauss (New York: NAL Trade, 2005).
- *When Your Child Has an Eating Disorder: A Step-by-Step Workbook for Parents and Other Caregivers,* by Abigail H. Natenshon (San Francisco: Jossey-Bass, 1999).

11
MENTAL DISORDERS

Mental illness is a term used for a group of disorders causing severe disturbances in thinking, feeling, and relating. The result is a diminished capacity for coping with the ordinary demands of life. Mental illnesses can affect persons of any age — children, adolescents, adults, the elderly — and they can occur in any family. Several million people in this country suffer from a serious, long-term mental illness.

Schizophrenia

Schizophrenia interferes with a person's ability to think clearly, distinguish reality from fantasy, manage emotions, make decisions, and relate to others. The first signs of schizophrenia typically emerge in the teenage years or early twenties. Schizophrenia is not caused by bad parenting or personal weakness. A person with schizophrenia does not have a "split personality," and almost all people with schizophrenia are not dangerous or violent toward others when they are receiving treatment. Schizophrenia is the most complex of the mental disorders.

Case Study

At age sixteen, Nikki was looking forward to getting her driver's license, dating, and having a lot more independence than she did when she was fifteen. She had been experiencing a few strange things for years but put them out of her mind until recently, when they became stronger and less easy to dismiss. She had been hearing voices she knew were not real, for example. Her family did not believe her when she told them about these voices, and so when the voices would speak, Nikki would just put them out of her mind. What was bothering her now was that she was sure people were plotting against her. She mentioned something to her best friend, Megan, and Megan thought she was kidding. Then Nikki noticed she was having difficulty maintaining conversations with people, and her friends were giving her strange looks when she was talking to them. She knew she was easily distracted, and it was hard to stay on topic, but this was the worst it had ever been. She couldn't seem to get things together. She would start a project, go to another, then another, back to the first, then to the next, back to the first, and never seem to be able to finish anything.

Signs and Symptoms

No one symptom positively identifies schizophrenia. All the symptoms of this illness can also be found in other brain disorders. People with schizophrenia may exhibit these symptoms:

- auditory hallucinations (hearing voices that are usually critical or threatening)
- visual hallucinations (seeing things that are not there)
- delusions (strong beliefs that are not in touch with reality, for example, people watching, harassing, or plotting against the person)
- disorganized speech (frequent off-topic conversations or speech that is not easily understood)
- disorganized behavior (difficulty planning and completing activities in an organized manner)

- confusion of fantasy and reality (unable to distinguish TV or movies from reality)
- catatonic behavior (unusual or bizarre behavior or sitting and staring as if paralyzed)
- reduction in emotional expression (lack of emotion when it is expected)
- lack of energy or motivation
- loss of enjoyment and interest in activities or social interaction
- extreme moodiness
- severe anxiety or fearfulness
- difficulty in performing schoolwork
- social withdrawal (serious problems in making and keeping friends)

Causes of schizophrenia are not known; however, if a family member has schizophrenia, the likelihood of other family members having it increases significantly. A combination of genetic factors along with environmental and behavioral factors is involved. The earlier the person is diagnosed and treated, the better the outcome.

Response, Diagnosis, and Treatment

To be accurately diagnosed with schizophrenia, the symptoms must be present for over a month, so it is important not to confuse short-term behaviors with long-term changes. Fear of what could occur next, denial of serious concerns, or fear of overreacting are common responses that need to be put aside if symptoms are present. When this disorder is suspected, it is imperative to notify the parents of the young person immediately. Professional help is the only appropriate treatment.

Schizophrenia is diagnosed by an interview with the young person and her parents. The core components of hallucinations or delusions need to be present. Disorganized speech and disorganized or catatonic behavior along with decreased functioning in academic or interpersonal relationships have to occur as well. The professional making the diagnosis will rule out other possible reasons for the changes in behavior and thought.

Treatment includes medication. When therapy is added to this treatment, results are generally quicker. Therapy consists of helping the person learn about the disorder and about coping strategies for dealing with it; teaching the person to differentiate between real and imagined voices; and helping the person implement lifestyle changes such as exercise, healthy eating, and sufficient sleep. Family therapy is often recommended to help the rest of the family learn how to deal with the disorder. Hospitalization is necessary at times when hallucinations or delusions are not helped with medication and when the person is unable to function appropriately in her environment.

Although there is no cure for schizophrenia, it is a highly treatable and manageable illness.

Depression

Unlike normal emotional experiences of sadness, loss, or passing mood states, major depression is persistent and can significantly interfere with an individual's thoughts, behavior, mood, activity, and physical health. Among the mood disorders, depression is the most common. Depression involves the whole person, including feelings, body, thoughts, and behaviors. It cannot be wished away or dismissed as a weakness. Depression can be lifelong or episodic; that is, it comes and goes for periods of time, or it occurs as a one-time event in a person's life.

Case Study

For fifteen-year-old Samantha, life was good. She had started her sophomore year in high school with friends she had known since elementary school. She was a good student and active in extracurricular activities. She and her sister were inseparable, and she was thinking nothing could ever happen that would upset her. She got along well with her parents, which was the envy of some of her friends. As the school year progressed, however, Samantha noticed she was more irritable than usual. She felt sad and empty. She was not interested in doing anything after school and had to force herself to get up in the morning just to go to school. After-school activities were no longer fun but tedious and boring. She withdrew from her sister and her parents, wanting to be alone in her room, out of communication with the family. She did not return phone calls from friends and was not interested in eating either at home or at school. She had begun to lose weight, which was unusual for her. She was not sleeping well, saying she just couldn't get to sleep at night. She felt sluggish and out of energy.

Signs and Symptoms

The onset of the first episode of depression may not be obvious if it is gradual or mild. The symptoms of depression include a significant change from how a person functioned before the illness. Here are some possible symptoms:

- persistent sad, anxious, or "empty" mood
- feelings of hopelessness or pessimism
- feelings of guilt, worthlessness, helplessness
- loss of interest or pleasure in usual activities
- withdrawal from family and friends
- sleep disturbance (oversleeping, not able to get to sleep, early morning awakening)
- eating disturbance (either loss or gain of weight and appetite)
- decreased energy, tiredness, sluggishness
- thoughts of death or suicide
- restlessness, irritability
- difficulty concentrating, remembering, making decisions
- physical symptoms such as headaches, digestive disorders, or chronic pain that are not affected by treatment

There is no single cause of major depression. Psychological, biological, and environmental factors may all contribute to its development. Whatever the specific causes of depression, scientific research has firmly established that depression is a biological brain disorder. Scientists have also found evidence of a genetic predisposition to depression. There is an increased risk for developing depression when there is a family history of the illness. Not everyone with a genetic predisposition develops depression, but some people probably have a biological makeup that leaves them particularly vulnerable to developing depression.

Life events—such as the death of a loved one, a major loss or change, chronic stress, and alcohol and drug abuse—may trigger episodes of depression. Some illnesses and some medications may also trigger depressive episodes. However, many depressive episodes occur spontaneously and are not triggered by a life crisis, physical illness, or other risks.

Response, Diagnosis, and Treatment

When working with young people, it is important to notice changes in their moods and behaviors. With adolescents it is particularly challenging because they seem to have mood swings all the time. However, when a person is noticeably different from how he used to be or is significantly different from his peers for a period of time, it is important to intervene. It is critical for adults to avoid making light of a young person's depressive feelings and to take them seriously. It is especially essential to realize the youth may be acting out of depression—not out of laziness, malice, or thoughtlessness—when tasks are not completed, enthusiasm is not present, or ideas are met with negativity. Letting parents know of concerns is the beginning of the process toward treatment.

Although depression can be a devastating illness, it is highly treatable. Depression is diagnosed through an interview conducted by a qualified professional with the young person and his parents. Some self-report questionnaires may be given to determine the intensity of the depressed feelings. If necessary, medication will be prescribed. In cases where the person is feeling suicidal or has made suicidal gestures, hospitalization is part of the treatment. If this is not necessary, outpatient appointments with a therapist are recommended to help the youth learn about depression, look at ways to cope with her depressive feelings, and learn ways of handling stress or other problems occurring in her life.

Bipolar Disorder

Bipolar disorder, or manic depression, is a serious brain disorder that causes extreme shifts in mood, energy, and functioning. In some cases, mood swings go from very low to very high. These highs are described as manic episodes. The person feels extremely happy, extremely energetic—the opposite of when he was feeling depressed. When these manic episodes are accompanied by depressive episodes, the person is said to have bipolar disorder.

Bipolar disorder is a chronic and generally lifelong condition with recurring episodes that often begin in adolescence or early adulthood. Generally those who suffer from bipolar disorder have symptoms of both mania and depression (sometimes at nearly the same time).

Case Study

Mike was used to getting sad on and off. He didn't think anything of it because he always seemed to be able to bounce back to his old self after a short time. Now that he was a senior, he was ready for graduation and moving on to exciting adventures at college—moving away from home, meeting new people, and starting a new life for himself. He felt in control of his life, but what he did not anticipate were these new feelings of high energy, talkativeness, and having multiple projects that he just couldn't finish. He found it easy to spend money and loved treating his friends with rides anywhere and anytime they wanted. He had difficulty concentrating and staying on task. When friends commented, he laughed and said he was just feeling excited about life and what lay ahead for him. But even he got concerned when everything seemed to come crashing down and he was more depressed than he had ever been. The depression seemed to come without warning and was more intense than before. At first he thought this was a one-time occurrence, but throughout the next few weeks, the cycle seemed to happen frequently. He no longer felt in control of any part of his life. He enjoyed the highs but was afraid of the lows.

Signs and Symptoms

Bipolar cycles vary from frequent to infrequent. They are different for young people than for adults in that the cycling from high to low can be more frequent, such as multiple times in a single day. In order to differentiate them from normal highs and lows, they must cause disturbance in functioning at home, at school, or with friends. In bipolar disorder, there is a cycling between depressive and manic episodes. *Mania* is the word that describes the activated phase of bipolar disorder. People experiencing mania may have the following symptoms:

- inflated self-esteem
- decreased need for sleep
- talkativeness (more than usual)
- thoughts that appear to be racing or coming faster than speech can manage
- distractibility (attention is easily given to unimportant external stimuli)
- increase in activity or feelings of restlessness
- excessive involvement in risk-taking activities, such as spending sprees or inappropriate sex
- mood changes that cannot be attributed to substance use or medication
- anger and aggressiveness (may be more evident in young people than in adults)
- rages lasting for hours without a trigger that would warrant such a response

Although the exact cause of bipolar disorder is not known, most researchers believe it is the result of a chemical imbalance in certain parts of the brain. Bipolar disorder tends to run in families, and close relatives of someone with bipolar disorder are more likely to be affected by the disorder. Sometimes life events such as a serious loss, chronic illness, illicit or prescription drug use, or other problems can trigger an episode in some individuals with a predisposition to the disorder. There are other possible triggers of bipolar episodes: the treatment of depression with an antidepressant medication may trigger a switch into mania, and sleep deprivation may trigger mania. It is important to note that bipolar episodes can and often do occur without any obvious trigger.

Response, Diagnosis, and Treatment

When an adult suspects a youth has bipolar disorder, it is essential that the parents are informed of the concerns. Because bipolar can be confused with a number of other disorders and is different from bipolar disorder in adults, the only accurate diagnosis can be made by a professional who is knowledgeable about bipolar disorder in young people. The professional obtains a history of the family and often includes questionnaires and interviews with the youth and the family in order to make a diagnosis.

Although bipolar disorder has no cure, it is a treatable and manageable illness. After an accurate diagnosis, most people can be successfully treated with medication. In addition, therapies including cognitive behavior therapy, interpersonal therapy, family therapy, and psychoeducation are important to help people understand the illness and to develop skills to cope with the stresses that can trigger episodes.

Pastoral Care Strategies

After youth have been identified as having schizophrenia, depression, or bipolar disorder, the adults in their life need to be extremely careful not to single them out as "crazy," "weird," or "misfit." These young people often feel isolated from others and are afraid of what others will think of them. This is particularly true if they have been hospitalized and will be returning to previous activities. Understanding their fears, helping them feel comfortable and accepted, especially by their peers (as well as helping their peers understand the disorder) are essential to integrating them into their peer groups.

In your own ministry to and with young people, keep these strategies in mind:

- Learn everything you can about mental illnesses.
- Be available for support and encouragement for young people and families dealing with mental illness.
- Invite professionals to speak on the various mental illnesses to help others understand the complexity of the disorders.
- Provide opportunities for support groups for youth and family members dealing with mental illnesses.
- Offer help to a family who is living with mental illness. Provide emotional support, understanding, and respite care for family members when needed.
- Object in writing and by telephone when mental illness is stigmatized publicly.
- Invite your parish or community colleagues to consider what your church is doing to make all persons with disabilities, including persons with mental illness, feel welcome and a part of community life.
- Advocate for youth with mental illnesses to help reduce stigma and increase information about the disorders.
- Discuss issues around mental illness and its effects on individuals, families, and communities.
- Support funding for research into severe mental illness.
- Contact the governor and your state representatives to let them know you care about services for persons who are mentally ill.
- Volunteer your help in programs serving persons who are mentally ill.
- Become active in the local chapter of the National Association of Mental Illness in order to receive current information and updates on progress in the treatment of schizophrenia, depression, and bipolar disorder.

Recommended Reading

- *The Bipolar Child: The Definitive and Reassuring Guide to Childhood's Most Misunderstood Disorder,* by Demitri and Janice Papolos (New York: Broadway Publishers, 2002).
- *The Day the Voices Stopped: A Schizophrenic's Journey from Madness to Hope,* by Ken Steele and Claire Berman (New York: Basic Books, 2002).
- *The Disappearing Girl: Learning the Language of Teenage Depression,* by Lisa Machoian (New York: Dutton Publishing, 2005).
- *I Am Not Sick! I Don't Need Help!* by Xavier Amador and Anna-Lica Johanson, PhD (Miami: Vida Publishing, 2000).
- *Surviving Manic Depression,* by E. Fuller Torrey and Michael B. Knable (New York: Basic Books, 2005).

12
BEHAVIOR DISORDERS

The most common behavior disorders found in the general population and described in the *Diagnostic and Statistical Manual of Mental Disorders* (DSM-IV-TR) include oppositional defiant disorder, attention-deficit/hyperactivity disorder, and conduct disorder.

Because diagnosis and treatment for all these disorders are essentially the same, this chapter includes the means of diagnosis and treatment at the end of the chapter instead of at the end of each section.

Oppositional Defiant Disorder

All young people are oppositional from time to time, particularly when tired, hungry, stressed, or upset. They may argue, talk back, disobey, and defy parents, teachers, and other adults. Oppositional behavior is often a normal part of development for young adolescents. However, openly uncooperative and hostile behavior becomes a serious concern when it is so frequent and consistent that it stands out when compared with other adolescents of the same age and developmental level and when it affects the young person's social, family, and academic life.

Case Study

Angie is fifteen. She has decent grades, but her teachers always say she is capable of much more. If they gave marks for getting along with others, it would be a different story. In the past, Angie would make a friend, smother her with attention, and that would be the end of it. Or the friend would not do exactly what Angie wanted, a big fight would ensue, and it would be over. But mostly Angie complained that everyone bugged her. What seemed to save Angie was the nursing home. Somewhere along the way, she got involved working there. To hear the staff there talk about her, you would never guess it was the same girl. Helpful, kind, thoughtful—they couldn't say enough good things about her. They figured it out when another teenager volunteered to help one of the same afternoons as Angie. Unfortunately the "other" Angie came out. She was tattling, annoying, disrespectful, and hard to get along with. Angie could get along with anyone, as long as they weren't her age, a teacher, or a relative!

Signs and Symptoms

Young people with oppositional defiant disorder (ODD) have an ongoing pattern of uncooperative, defiant, and hostile behavior toward authority figures that seriously interferes with their day to day functioning. Symptoms of ODD may include the following:

- frequent temper tantrums
- excessive arguing with adults
- active defiance and refusal to comply with adult requests and rules
- deliberate attempts to annoy or upset people
- blaming others for one's own mistakes or misbehavior
- easily annoyed by others, touchy
- frequent anger and resentment
- mean and hateful talking when upset
- revenge seeking

ODD might be described as a "will not" disorder. The young person can do what is asked of him but chooses not to. A child with this disorder tests the patience of those around him, is unwilling to do what is asked, argues about insignificant details, and is easily angered himself.

Attention-Deficit/Hyperactivity Disorder

Any young person may show inattention, distractibility, impulsivity, or hyperactivity at times, but the young person with attention-deficit/hyperactivity disorder shows these symptoms and behaviors more frequently and severely than others of the same age or developmental level.

Case Study

David is a thirteen-year-old eighth grade student who has reading and math skills one to two years below grade level. He is failing every subject and seems destined to repeat the eighth grade. His teachers describe him as disruptive in class and have said he has difficulty paying attention during structured and unstructured activities. More often than not, David has trouble finishing what he starts, cannot follow through when given instructions, and has schoolwork that is disorganized, messy, and careless. David also has difficulty waiting his turn in class. His teachers describe him as having low self-esteem, poor frustration tolerance, and unstable mood swings.

Signs and Symptoms

A young person with ADHD often displays some of the following symptoms:
- trouble paying attention
- inattentive to details, makes careless mistakes
- easily distracted

- loses school supplies, forgets to turn in homework
- trouble finishing class work and homework
- trouble listening
- trouble following multiple adult commands
- impulsive, blurts out answers
- impatient
- fidgets or squirms
- leaves seat and runs about or climbs excessively
- seems "on the go"
- talks too much and has difficulty being quiet
- interrupts or intrudes on others

ADHD is found in children of all ages, and many young people diagnosed with ADHD will continue to have significant symptoms into adulthood. It's important to note that most children with ADHD also have ODD. ADHD is known to be a genetic disorder. Often children whose parents have depression, bipolar disorder, or anxiety disorder are diagnosed with ADHD at young ages. Sometimes these same children have bipolar disorder when they are older.

Attention-deficit/hyperactivity disorder might be called a "cannot" disorder; that is, the person with ADHD is unable to or cannot concentrate, sit still, reduce impulsivity, and manage her behavior without intervention.

Conduct Disorder

Conduct disorder is a complicated group of behavioral and emotional problems in children and adolescents. People with this disorder have great difficulty following rules and behaving in a socially acceptable way. They are often viewed by their peers, adults, and social agencies as "bad" or delinquent rather than mentally ill.

Case Study

Joseph is fourteen. Joseph's mother hated school almost as much as he did. Almost every day the school called about Joseph. In preschool he tried to stab a child with a pair of scissors. He was swearing at his teachers by the first grade. Every time they seemed to get one problem under control, he was into something else. He refused to do any homework from fourth grade on. Up until that grade, his teachers let him go out for a walk around the building every hour or so, but when a set of keys went missing and were "discovered" by Joseph a few days later, the walks ended. Joseph was suspended from seventh grade when he threw a match into a boy's locker. Why did Joseph do it? The boy had called him stupid. Joseph was out for a week; then after only two days back, he was thrown out for making death threats against his teacher. Then Joseph was arrested for vandalizing the school.

Signs and Symptoms

Children or adolescents with conduct disorder may exhibit some of the following behaviors:
- aggressive or physically cruel to people and animals
- bullies, threatens, or intimidates others
- often initiates physical fights
- uses a weapon that could cause serious physical harm to others
- steals from a victim while confronting them (for example, assault)
- forces someone into sexual activity
- destroys property
- sets fires with the intention to cause damage
- deliberately destroys others' property
- breaks into someone else's building, house, or car
- lies to obtain goods or favors, or to avoid obligations
- shoplifts
- seriously violates rules
- stays out at night despite parental objections
- runs away from home
- skips school

Conduct disorder is often found in youth who have parents with poor boundaries and who disrespect the rights of others. Young people with conduct disorder frequently are not disciplined or have extremely strict discipline in their homes. This disorder is more common with males than females. Boys with the disorder often have little contact with their fathers or have been abused by them.

Young people with this disorder are challenging because sometimes they simply do not care about consequences. There is a definite difference between children who occasionally get into fights, steal a candy bar, or tease others. Young people with conduct disorder do these activities routinely and do not necessarily feel any guilt about causing fear or pain to others.

Youth with conduct disorder are recognizable by their lack of respect over time. They can usually be counted on to be disagreeable, involved in fights or arguments, untrustworthy, intimidating, and bullying. They tend to have few friends and are feared by their peers. There is a continuum of severity with this disorder. The range is from mild with few problems to severe with many problems or causing considerable harm to others. Many factors contribute to a young person developing conduct disorder, including brain damage, child abuse, genetic vulnerability, school failure, and traumatic life experiences.

Response, Diagnosis, and Treatment

A young person who exhibits symptoms of a behavior disorder should be examined by a physician or mental health specialist, who will talk with the young person and his or her parents and review the young person's medical history. Sometimes other medical tests are necessary as well.

Treatment may include parent training programs to help manage the young person's behavior, individual and family psychotherapy to improve communication, cognitive behavior therapy, and social skills training. Without proper treatment, the young person may fall behind in school, and relationships may suffer.

Other treatment includes modifications to the young person's education program. Behavior therapy can help a young person control aggression, modulate social behavior, and be more productive.

Cognitive therapy can help a young person build self-esteem, reduce negative thoughts, and improve problem-solving skills. Parents can learn behavior management skills, for example, issuing instructions one step at a time rather than issuing multiple requests at once. Treatment may also include medication. Treatment is rarely brief because establishing new attitudes and behavior patterns takes time. However, early treatment offers a young person a better chance for considerable improvement and hope for a more successful future.

Pastoral Care Strategies

When young people understand they are more than their disorder or disability, they will be able to feel accepted and use their strengths to their advantage. Youth with behavior disorders benefit from having choices. These choices need to be such that each choice is acceptable. One example would be, "Would you like to sit in the front of the room near me, or next to the door near the assistant?" The best way to approach a young person with behavior disorders and to avoid a power struggle is to offer choices.

In your own ministry to and with young people, keep these strategies in mind:

- Always build on the positives; give young people praise and positive reinforcement when they show flexibility or cooperation.
- Take a time-out or break if you are about to make the conflict with the young person worse, not better. This is good modeling for a young person.
- Support the young person who decides to take a time-out to prevent overreacting.
- Set up reasonable, age-appropriate limits with consequences that can be enforced consistently. Be certain to have parental support for these consequences.
- Listen to all young people's requests, give reasons for your opinions, listen to their opinions, and negotiate. *Communication, negotiation,* and *compromise* will prove helpful.

- Reduce seating distractions. Lessening distractions might be as simple as seating a young person near you or another leader instead of near a window.
- Post the schedule in a prominent place so the young people can see where they are expected to be and when.
- Instead of long-winded explanations and cajoling, use clear, brief directions to remind young people of their responsibilities.
- Use a chart to list goals and track positive behaviors. Then reward the efforts. Be sure the goals are realistic (think baby steps rather than overnight success).
- Use time-outs or removal of privileges as consequences for inappropriate behavior.
- Find out what each young person does well and recognize him for it. Success can boost social skills and self-esteem.
- Give young people only one set of directions at a time. Keep instructions clear and brief, breaking down larger tasks into smaller, more manageable pieces.
- Allow young people the space to move around, if necessary, or give them tasks that allow free movement.

Recommended Reading

- *All the Best Answers for the Worst Kid Problems: Antisocial Youth and Conduct Disorders,* by Ruth Herman Wells (Woodburn, OR: Youth Change, 2003).
- *The Defiant Child: A Parent's Guide to Oppositional Defiant Disorder,* by Douglas Riley (Lanham, MD: Taylor Trade Publishing, 1997).
- *Driven to Distraction: Recognizing and Coping with Attention Deficit Disorder from Childhood Through Adulthood,* by Edward M. Hallowell and John J. Ratey (New York: Touchstone, 1995).
- *Kids in the Syndrome Mix of ADHD, LD, Asperger's, Tourette's, Bipolar, and More: The One-Stop Guide for Parents, Teachers, and Other Professionals,* by Martin L. Kutscher, MD, and Tony Attwood, PhD (London: Jessica Kingsley Publishers, 2005).
- *Taking Charge of ADHD: The Complete, Authoritative Guide for Parents,* by Russell A. Barkley (New York: The Guilford Press, 2000).

13
ANXIETY DISORDERS

Anxiety disorders are recognized as causing excess fear, distress, and uneasy feelings that others would not experience under similar circumstances. They are treatable, and when recognized and treated early, a lifetime of needless suffering can be prevented. However, owing to shame and possible stigma, many people do not seek help and attempt to cover up the symptoms, reducing the possibility of getting the help they need.

Post-Traumatic Stress Disorder

Post-traumatic stress disorder can occur in young people who have experienced or witnessed life-threatening events such as natural disasters, serious accidents, terrorist incidents, war, or violent personal assaults like rape. It was originally thought to be a disorder of veterans of war, but it is now known to affect people who have experienced other life-threatening events or seen others in situations that appear to be life threatening.

Case Study

When Mark was fifteen, he was described as "remarkably healthy." He had no problems with appetite, sleep, or getting along with others. He had no fears about anything, including new or risky situations. About a month after his sixteenth birthday, he and three friends were celebrating his getting his driver's license. They decided they would drive out of town into a new area to explore what was outside their usual territory. Enroute, an oncoming car lost control, hitting Mark's car head on. The front passengers survived the crash. One of the boys in the back had not fastened his seatbelt and flew through the windshield; he was killed instantly. Mark did not remember much of the crash except for the noise, the blood, and his friend's body in the ditch. The other driver and his passenger were killed, and Mark remembered seeing them and their car as a gruesome tangle of metal, glass, bodies, and blood. Mark physically recovered from his injuries without major problems. However, after he was discharged from the hospital and after his friend's funeral, he seemed to be an entirely different person. He did not want to drive or even get in a car again. He could not sleep at night, complaining of nightmares and fear of falling asleep. He would often have flashbacks of the accident, seeing the scene replayed in his mind repeatedly. He did not want to talk about the accident. He knew it was not his fault, but he seemed to question why he lived and his friend did not. When he heard sirens, he relived the accident as though it were happening again and again. He was unwilling to spend time with the other boys who were in the accident. He withdrew and was unable to concentrate in school. He appeared sad and morose. He did not want to attend social activities and instead chose to be alone. His grades plummeted, he was angry much of the time, he lost a significant amount of weight, and his friends were concerned he might become suicidal.

Signs and Symptoms

Symptoms of post-traumatic stress disorder (PTSD) fall into three general categories: intrusion, avoidance, and hyperarousal. Intrusion involves unwanted thoughts entering the mind of the person. Avoidance affects relationships with others. Hyperarousal causes people to act as if they are re-experiencing the threat of the trauma. PTSD may include these symptoms:

- recurrent and intrusive distressing recollections of the event, including images, thoughts, or perceptions
- distressing dreams of the event
- acting or believing that the traumatic event is recurring
- intense anxiety and distress from exposure to situations resembling the traumatic event
- body reactivity on exposure to situations resembling the traumatic event
- avoidance of thoughts, feelings, or conversations associated with the trauma
- avoidance of activities, places, or people that remind one of the traumatic event
- inability to remember details of the event
- markedly diminished participation and interest in usual activities
- feelings of detachment and estrangement from others
- restricted range of emotional expression
- sense of a foreshortened future or lifespan
- difficulty falling asleep or staying asleep
- irritability or anger outbursts
- difficulty concentrating
- excessive vigilance
- exaggerated startle response

Depression often accompanies unresolved PTSD symptoms. PTSD can occur at any age, including early childhood. The symptoms are relieved within three months in about half of the cases, according to the DSM-IV-TR (p. 466). Others may have symptoms that persist over a long period of time, up to years. The symptoms may come and go, and may return after a period when there has been exposure to another event similar to the original trauma.

Response, Diagnosis, and Treatment

Because professional treatment is necessary when PTSD is present over a period of time, it is essential to recommend treatment to the young person's parents. The youth may not be willing to accept help, and if this is so, the parents would benefit from talking to a professional about how to help their son or daughter or to get their child help despite his protests.

PTSD is diagnosed by a mental health professional, who obtains a complete history of the youth and his family. This is necessary to determine what is typical in the family as well as what changes have occurred since the trauma was experienced. The person is asked to describe the trauma, if possible. If it is too difficult, the professional will be able to determine the extent of the trauma from the responses and reactions to the questions asked as well as the behaviors that have changed since the trauma.

Cognitive behavior therapy (CBT) may be used to change the painful and intrusive patterns of behavior and thought by teaching relaxation techniques and looking at the thoughts that may be causing further trauma. Exposure therapy uses methods of re-introducing the trauma and allowing the person to experience the feelings in a safe environment so he can face and gain control of the fear that was overwhelming at the time of the trauma. Family therapy may be used to help the rest of the family cope with the changes in their lives because of the trauma. Group therapy or support groups may be used to help survivors share their stories and obtain support from others with similar experiences. Medication is also effective, particularly when the responses to the trauma are debilitating and leave the person unable to function in his environment.

Obsessive-Compulsive Disorder

Worries, doubts, and superstitious beliefs are common in everyday life. However, when they become excessive, such as hours of hand washing, or make no sense at all, such as driving around and around the block to check that an accident hasn't occurred, then a diagnosis of OCD is made. In OCD it is as though the brain gets stuck on a particular thought or urge and just can't let go.

Case Study

At age thirteen, Laura knew she was different from the other kids around her. She was able to hide most of the thoughts that plagued her, and if she was really careful, she thought no one would notice she had to have things in a specific order around her. She hoped people would think she was just extra neat. She was anxious much of the time, as was her mother and her maternal grandmother. She could calm the fears of impending doom and harm coming to her family members by arranging her environment. She would put her books in ascending or descending order on the bookshelves. Her pencils were stacked with longer ones on the bottom. Her stuffed animals were arranged by color and size. Her crayons were always in the box and put in according to size—bigger ones in the back and smaller ones in the front. She knew it probably didn't make any difference, but she didn't want to take the chance that if she didn't do the ordering, her parents might be killed on the way home from work, or her sister might be hit by a car on the way home from school. Laura had tried to stop the behaviors, but the anxiety about harm to her family increased so tremendously she had to continue. After all, how would she feel if something happened and she hadn't done her ordering routine?

If Laura couldn't get her environment in order, she counted. She would count silently, so no one would know. Counting and ordering seemed to make a difference, and she was not about to stop. What she was noticing, however, was that the ordering and counting were increasing, and she wasn't sure how much longer she could keep it a secret. Her friends were beginning to make comments about how orderly everything had to be, and Laura was afraid they would find out soon. Besides, she was having a hard time concentrating in school when the thoughts would come and she would have to straighten something out or count the number of people in each row or the number of desks in the room. It was also getting harder to get everything done when she had to interrupt her work to order or count. Maybe her mother would be able to help her figure out what to do. It probably would be worth asking her because Laura knew her mother talked about how worrying seemed to run in their family.

Signs and Symptoms

Symptoms of OCD are persistent, repetitive, nonpleasurable behaviors associated with anxiety. The person often is aware that the thoughts and behaviors are excessive or unreasonable but is unable to stop them. In younger children, that awareness may not be present, but with adolescents and adults, the range of awareness varies considerably.

Obsessions are thoughts, images, or impulses that occur over and over again and feel out of control. The person does not want to have these ideas, finds them disturbing and intrusive, and usually recognizes they don't really make sense. People with OCD may worry excessively about dirt and germs and be obsessed with the idea they are contaminated or may contaminate others. Or they may have obsessive fears of having inadvertently harmed someone else (perhaps while pulling the car out of the driveway), even though they usually know this is not realistic. Obsessions are accompanied by uncomfortable feelings, such as fear, disgust, doubt, or a sensation that things have to be done in a way that is "just so." Here are some common obsessions:

- contamination fears of germs, dirt, and so on
- imagining having harmed self or others
- imagining losing control or acting on aggressive urges
- intrusive sexual thoughts or urges
- excessive religious or moral doubt
- forbidden thoughts
- a need to have things "just so"

- a need to tell, ask, confess

(Obsessive-Compulsive Foundation Web site)

People with OCD typically try to make their obsessions go away by performing compulsions. Compulsions are acts the person performs over and over again, often according to certain "rules." For example, people with an obsession about contamination may wash constantly to the point their hands become raw and inflamed. OCD compulsions do not give the person pleasure; rather, the rituals are performed to obtain relief from the discomfort caused by the obsessions. Common compulsions include these:

- washing
- repeating
- checking
- touching
- counting
- arranging or ordering
- hoarding or saving
- praying

(Obsessive-Compulsive Foundation Web site)

OCD symptoms cause distress, take up a lot of time (more than an hour a day), or significantly interfere with the person's school and work life, social life, or relationships. OCD usually begins in adolescence but can begin in childhood. For boys it is seen earlier than for girls. Onset is usually gradual, with symptoms coming and going, particularly in times of stress. There is a higher incidence of OCD in individuals when other family members also have OCD (DSM-IV-TR, p. 460).

Response, Diagnosis, and Treatment

Telling the person who has obsessions or compulsions to stop because her behavior is illogical or nonsensical is futile. Letting her know this is a difficult situation for her and supporting her in her attempts to eliminate the thoughts and behaviors is a better response. Informing the young person's parents of your concerns in order for her to obtain treatment is essential. Letting the young person know treatment is not only available but effective may help her break down her resistance to getting help. Also telling her this is a common disorder and that she is not alone is also helpful.

The disorder is diagnosed by a professional who is familiar with OCD symptoms. Diagnosis is made by learning the family history and asking questions about thoughts and behaviors as well as the duration of symptoms. How the thoughts and behaviors affect everyday functioning is part of determining the extent of the disorder. Treatment includes cognitive behavior therapy, which focuses on resolving conflicts and stressors. Behavior therapy uses techniques such as guided imagery, relaxation training, and "flooding." Flooding is based on the theory that anxiety usually decreases after repeated contact with something feared. For example, people with obsessions about germs are told to stay in contact with "germy" objects (for example, handling money) until their anxiety is relieved. Their anxiety tends to decrease after repeated exposure until they no longer fear the contact. For flooding to be most helpful, it needs to be combined with response or ritual prevention (RP). In RP, the person's rituals or avoidance behaviors are blocked. For example, those with excessive worries about germs must not only stay in contact with germy things but must also refrain from ritualized washing.

Medication is often effective in helping the person relax enough to be able to change the behaviors and thinking while other therapies are being worked on. Changing habits is helpful by reducing caffeine intake, getting adequate sleep, reducing stressors, and getting support from others.

Generalized Anxiety Disorder

Generalized anxiety disorder (GAD) is much more than the normal anxiety people experience day to day. It's chronic and exaggerated worry and tension, even though nothing seems to provoke it. Having this disorder means always anticipating disaster, often worrying excessively about health, money, family, school, or work. Sometimes, though, the source of the worry is hard to pinpoint. Simply the thought of getting through the day provokes anxiety.

Case Study

Ben had always been a worrier according to his friends. Now that he was fifteen, he was getting concerned because he wanted to quit worrying but had never been able to. He told his friends he didn't want to worry; it was just a part of who he was. But he wanted it to change. He noticed no one worried about things like he did. If he had a test coming up, he worried days ahead of time. If he said something he didn't like, he worried about it for days afterward. He was worried about how he would do in sports before the season had begun. He found the worrying to be exhausting. He could not sleep at night, and he was irritable and restless much of the time. It took a lot of effort for him to concentrate on his assignments and not on worrying about something else. Now that he was nearing adulthood, he wanted a different life for himself. He was determined to do whatever it took to make that change happen.

Signs and Symptoms

People with GAD can't seem to shake their concerns, even though they usually realize their anxiety is more intense than the situation warrants. People with GAD also seem unable to relax. To qualify as a disorder, generalized anxiety disorder must be present for at least six months. People with generalized anxiety disorder (GAD) may have the following symptoms:

- restlessness or feeling keyed up or on edge
- fatigue
- difficulty concentrating or mind going blank
- irritability
- muscle tension, including trembling, twitching, muscle aches, and soreness

- sleep disturbance (difficulty falling or staying asleep or restless, unsatisfying sleep)
- somatic complaints, including headaches, nausea, diarrhea
- exaggerated startle response

The disorder is found more frequently in females than males. There may be a genetic component to GAD; individuals with a family history of GAD are more likely to be diagnosed with the disorder.

Response, Diagnosis, and Treatment

Professional assistance is the first step to getting help with this disorder. Because it ebbs and flows for long periods, individuals may think it has gone, but it may reappear again when least expected or when stress is high. Informing parents of concerns about the disorder's presence in a youth's behaviors is important. Because the person has difficulty controlling the worry, arguing with him and telling him there is nothing to worry about is not effective. If it were that easy, he probably would have quit worrying a long time ago. However, having an understanding attitude and recognizing the difficulty despite the lack of logic in the behavior will provide support and decrease the anxiety.

Generalized anxiety disorder is diagnosed by a professional who is able to distinguish GAD from other anxiety disorders. It is important to make this distinction because treatment for other disorders may be different. The professional obtains a family history and asks questions about frequency, duration, and intensity of the anxiety.

Generalized anxiety has been shown to respond best to cognitive behavior therapy, an active therapy that involves more than just talking to a therapist. In CBT, the person gradually learns to see situations and problems in a different perspective and learns methods and techniques to alleviate and reduce anxiety. Sometimes medication is helpful to therapy, but for many people it is not necessary. Research indicates that generalized anxiety is fully treatable and can be successfully overcome in three to four months if the person is motivated and works toward recovery.

Panic Disorder

Panic disorder usually appears during the teens or early adulthood years, and though the exact causes are unclear, there does seem to be a connection with major life transitions that are potentially stressful. Panic disorder is one of the more unusual anxiety disorders in that it consists of panic attacks that are sudden, discrete episodes of intense fear and discomfort along with either bodily or cognitive symptoms. These symptoms peak within ten minutes, then often subside entirely within twenty to thirty minutes. Following a panic attack, the person has an intense fear of having another one.

Case Study

Erik remembered exactly when his first panic attack occurred. He was sitting in math class in his sophomore year when, for no apparent reason, he began to feel like he was dying. His breath quickened, he felt extremely hot, he began sweating, he thought he was going to choke, and he wanted to leave immediately but was too afraid he would pass out or die. He stayed where he was for a while and within a few minutes the sensations stopped and he felt normal again. This scared him a lot, and he became afraid of being in math class. He asked the teacher if he could change his seat so he could be by a door in case he had another attack. He figured it worked because nothing like that happened again for many months. Then one day in choir, the symptoms repeated themselves. He felt lightheaded, like he was going crazy, and had tingling sensations throughout his body. This time he was close to a door, so he left quickly and sat down in the hallway to clear his head. Now he was not so sure this wouldn't happen again. He thought maybe he could be in regular classrooms with chairs instead of classes where he stood most of the time, such as choir. He decided to drop choir and sit near the door in other classes. His fear of having another attack became his number one thought. Anytime his heart began to race, he would get scared. The attacks were unexpected and terrifying beyond anything he had ever experienced. It was the closest he ever felt to dying, and his primary response was to avoid anything that would likely cause another attack to happen.

Over time the fear of another attack intensified, even though Erik rarely had other attacks. The fear took on a life of its own, and Erik spent most of his time either avoiding places he thought might trigger an attack or thinking about what he would do if another attack occurred. His concentration was not good, his interactions with peers were poor, and his willingness to try new things or even do familiar activities decreased immensely.

Signs and Symptoms

The intensity of the anxiety that occurs with panic attacks differentiates it from other forms of anxiety. This intensity is different from fear that occurs when one is anxious under normal circumstances. It is out of the realm of common experience, which is the reason the attempts to avoid the attacks take on such a priority. People with panic disorder may have some or all of the following symptoms:
- heart palpitations or fast heart rate
- sweating
- trembling or shaking
- shortness of breath or smothering
- choking sensation
- chest discomfort or pain
- nausea or abdominal distress
- dizziness, lightheadedness, or unsteadiness
- feelings of unreality or being detached from oneself
- fear of losing control or going crazy
- fear of dying
- numbness or tingling sensations
- chills or hot flashes
- worry about having other panic attacks
- marked changes in behavior related to the panic attacks

Many times a person with panic disorder also has another anxiety disorder. When there is a family history of panic attacks, the likelihood of an individual having panic disorder increases significantly.

Response, Diagnosis, and Treatment

Because panic disorders are so frightening and the possibility of avoidance of perceived triggers is so debilitating, it is critical that a person receive treatment as soon as symptoms are acknowledged. Because the symptoms may wax and wane over time, it may seem as though they are gone for good and will not return. However, they may return with devastating effects for the person involved. Diagnosis is made by a professional who obtains a family history and a description of the symptoms. The symptoms are compared to symptoms of other anxiety disorders to determine which disorder is most prominent or which may also be present with the panic disorder.

Treatment includes education on ways to identify and change thought patterns that perpetuate fear. The person learns to identify the thoughts that come automatically that may trigger physical feelings of panic, and he tries to change these thoughts to be more realistic. Exposure therapy helps the youth learn specific ways of reducing his fear of the anxious feelings. The youth also learns to use skills to go to situations that previously were avoided or feared, and he practices different ways of coping with the fears. These skills might be reinforced by parents or other trusted adults who can coach the young person through his fears.

Social Phobia

Social phobia, unlike shyness, is a fear of being humiliated or embarrassed in social situations. Whereas shy children are uneasy in new situations or in social situations, youth with social phobia will avoid any situation that involves being seen or noticed by others. They fear ridicule and are afraid of looking foolish. Just like with other phobias, this fear is out of proportion to the actual danger that is present. A person with social phobia usually overrates the danger of embarrassment while underrating her ability to get through the situation. Social phobia is disruptive to a normal life and interferes with school, friendships, and social interactions.

Case Study

Sara was not exactly sure when she noticed she was becoming increasingly more anxious around others. She had always been shy, but now that she was in middle school, she noticed it was getting much worse. Instead of just being uncomfortable around people, she was avoiding them altogether. When school activities were being planned, she was visibly anxious. She was increasingly anxious about being with her peers. When she was supposed to give a report to her class, she became so upset the night before that she was nauseous and unable to sleep. The day of the report she felt unable to stand up because she was so shaky and lightheaded. She knew she was overreacting and needed to use her coping skills, but they did not seem to be working anymore. The teacher was patient, but it was not enough. Sara could not give the report and did not want to return to school. She thought maybe a couple days at home would help her feel better, but as each day passed, she was more reluctant to return. The thought of going into the school was as anxiety-producing as attempting to give the report had been.

Signs and Symptoms

Social phobia usually begins in the mid-teens but can begin as early as childhood. It usually follows a history of social inhibition or shyness. It can start with a particularly humiliating experience or may begin slowly and evolve into extreme anxiety around people. It can disappear for a while and return after many years. People with social phobia may exhibit the following symptoms:
• persistent fear of one or more situations in which a person is

exposed to unfamiliar people or scrutiny by others
- fear of appearing foolish or doing something that would invite ridicule from others
- fear of going to social events
- fear of talking with authority figures such as a teacher or principal
- fear of speaking to others in public
- fear of using a public restroom
- fear of eating out or talking on the phone
- fear of writing on the chalkboard in front of peers
- avoidance of situations or activities that involve being with others
- recognition that the fear is excessive or unreasonable (this awareness may not be present in all youth)

To be diagnosed as social phobia, the duration of the symptoms needs to be more than six months and needs to cause impairment in functioning. It is also significant that this behavior is a change from previous functioning and that relationships had been able to be established and maintained prior to the extreme anxiety. Social phobia is more common in women than in men. There is a higher likelihood of the disorder being present in an individual who has a family history of social phobia.

Response, Diagnosis, and Treatment

Patience is critical with youth suffering from social phobia. Professional intervention is required to help the young person learn coping skills to conquer her fears. Applying logic or consequences rarely is effective because the fear of being humiliated or embarrassed is more intense than the fear of the consequence.

The disorder is diagnosed when a professional obtains a family history and interviews the youth and her parents. Questions about intensity, frequency, and duration of symptoms help differentiate among the various anxiety disorders. Treatment includes teaching appropriate social skills, learning to identify and change negative thoughts that increase feelings of anxiety in social situations, and learning to think more positive, rational thoughts in order to engage in social situations more readily. Cognitive therapy helps reduce distorted thinking by teaching which thoughts are inappropriate and changeable. Helping the young person identify what situations are challenging and then teaching her specific coping skills to deal with those situations also is part of therapy. Parents might be involved in the sessions to educate them about anxiety. They can be used as coaches who help their young person apply the skills between sessions. Group therapy can enable the youth to interact with others, realize she is not alone, and learn skills from peers. Medication can reduce the anxiety and allow the youth to better participate in therapy.

Pastoral Care Strategies

Anxiety can be crippling, but it does not have to be so with appropriate treatment, acceptance, and support from those who are around these youth. As with other problems, once the youth can recognize the symptoms, feel accepted for who they are, and know they will be able to succeed in showing improvement, the sooner they will be able to overcome the odds against them and be healthy and active in their life situations. In your own ministry to and with young people, keep these strategies in mind:
- Educate yourself on all aspects of anxiety disorders.
- Keep an open mind to information that may be emotionally difficult to hear.
- Never require a young person to stand in front of a crowd or share information that might make her uncomfortable. Always ask for volunteers—don't "designate."
- Advocate for speakers on the topic of anxiety disorders and their effects on the well-being and development of youth.
- Invite adults who have conquered anxiety disorders to be role models for youth who are struggling to learn coping skills.
- Be available for support and encouragement of youth who are in

need.

- Provide tips for parents to keep the lines of communication with their children open. Alert parents and other caregivers to common signs of anxiety disorders.
- When a tragedy or trauma occurs in the life of a young person or his family, provide the family with resources for sharing and praying together.
- Respond to false statements about mental illness or people with mental illnesses. Many people have wrong and damaging ideas on the subject. Accurate facts and information may help change both their ideas and actions.
- Work with local schools or other youth-serving organizations to develop education programs about mental illness, or establish a prevention program for at-risk young people.
- Locate a mental health professional to assist in the development of a peer-to-peer support group for young people with serious mental illness who are interested in establishing and maintaining their wellness and recovery.

Recommended Reading

- *Anxiety Disorders: Everything You Need to Know,* by Paul J. Caldwell, MD (Tonawanda, NY: Firefly Books, 2005).
- *Loving Someone with OCD: Help for You and Your Family,* by Karen J. Landsman, Kathleen M. Rupertus, and Cherry Pedrick (Oakland, CA: New Harbinger Publications, 2005).
- *Panic Disorder and Anxiety in Adolescence,* by Sara Golden Mattis and Thomas H. Ollendick (Maiden, MA: Blackwell Publishing, 2002).
- *Post-Traumatic Stress Disorder Sourcebook,* by Glenn R. Schiraldi (New York: McGraw-Hill, 2000).

14
IMPULSE CONTROL DISORDERS

As their name implies, impulse control disorders involve a recurrent failure to resist impulsive behaviors that harm oneself or others. According to the DSM-IV-TR (p. 663), there are five conditions diagnosable as impulse control disorders. These include intermittent explosive disorder, kleptomania, pyromania, pathological gambling, and trichotillomania (recurrent pulling out of one's hair). Pathological gambling was discussed in the section on addictions. Pyromania is a fascination with fire setting. It involves the deliberate and purposeful setting of fires on more than one occasion. In addition to these disorders, another disorder that is not included in the DSM-IV-TR but is considered by some experts as a type of impulse control disorder is self-mutilation, which involves cutting, scratching, or burning oneself. Generally speaking, impulse control disorders cannot be prevented. They are usually rare in isolation, most often found in combination with other disorders. Exact causes are unknown but may be connected to genetics, environment, or neurological factors.

Because diagnosis and treatment for impulse control disorders are essentially the same, this chapter includes the means of diagnosis and treatment at the end of the chapter instead of at the end of each section as done in other chapters.

Intermittent Explosive Disorder

Intermittent explosive disorder (IED) is a mental disturbance characterized by specific episodes of violent and aggressive behavior that may involve harm to others, harm to oneself, or destruction of property. Usually these episodes follow minor incidents and are out of proportion to the trigger. The young person may describe the episodes as "spells" or "attacks" in which the explosive behavior is preceded by a sense of tension or arousal and followed immediately by a sense of relief. Often genuine regret is expressed after the outburst. Later the young person may also feel upset, remorseful, or embarrassed about the behavior.

Case Study

At age sixteen, Justin had a history of angry outbursts. He often said he didn't feel in control of his anger. He got into frequent fights at school over seemingly meaningless events. He appeared to overreact to minor incidents and felt terribly remorseful afterward. He was feeling especially good now because he had a girlfriend, his first. His parents did not allow him to date until he was sixteen, and he had been looking forward to this privilege for at least two years. He thought about Mariah almost all the time. They had a lot of fun together, and he was sure she would never make him angry and he would never get into an argument with her. He was hopeful his reputation as a guy who could get into fights easily would now change forever. And for a long time he was calm.

However, when he and Mariah were out one evening, she said something that really triggered his anger. He yelled at her, called her names, threatened to hurt her, and scared her a lot. He began hitting on his car, broke off the outside mirror, and threw it, shattering it to pieces. Mariah said she wanted to go home, and at that point Justin knew he had to be away from her. When he dropped her off at her house, she was crying uncontrollably; she said she didn't want to see him again and would call the police if he didn't stay away from her.

Justin was devastated. He didn't want this to happen. He didn't want to lose Mariah. He didn't want to go back to his old behaviors. But here he was and he didn't know how he got here. His dad had been warning him for years that he would regret having such a temper, but nothing anyone had said or done previously had been helpful.

Signs and Symptoms

Intermittent explosive disorder is marked by several episodes of failure to resist aggressive impulses that result in serious assaults or destruction of property. Young people with IED sometimes describe intense impulses to be aggressive before their aggressive acts. People with intermittent explosive disorder may have the following symptoms:

- inability to control angry and aggressive impulses
- violent behavior, such as physical assault, destruction of property, and homicide or violent suicide
- violence that cannot be accounted for by any other mental or physical condition
- physiological symptoms with the aggression, such as tingling, buildup of pressure inside the head or chest, and heart palpitations
- exhaustion or deflated mood after the aggression

The majority of cases occur when an individual is between late adolescence and the late twenties. There is some evidence that the neurotransmitter serotonin may play a role in this disorder. Although the prevalence of intermittent explosive disorder is unknown yet considered rare, the disorder is probably more common than realized and may be an important cause of violent behavior. Intermittent explosive disorder is more common in males and in families with mood disorders or substance abuse.

Kleptomania

Kleptomania involves the failure to resist impulses to steal things that are not needed either for personal use or for their monetary value.

There is typically anxiety before the theft and relief or gratification afterward. Kleptomania is quite rare, whereas common shoplifting is not. Kleptomania is different from shoplifting because of the impulsivity and lack of gain from the theft. The impulsivity increases the likelihood of getting caught because there is no thought about the consequences; the goal is to relieve the anxiety and the strong urge to steal.

Case Study

Heather was fourteen, had a stable family, and was able to ask her parents for almost anything she wanted and they would give it to her. She had good friends and was a good student. On the exterior, she seemed to have everything—good looks, good family, brains, and friends. She was perplexed when she had strong urges to take things from stores. The urges were strong, but the items she chose to steal were insignificant. At first when she did not get caught she was relieved, and the urges seemed to subside. As time went on, however, the urges got stronger and she was finding herself in the middle of a mess. She had learned how to take things without getting caught, and no one knew about the urges. She had told no one—not even her best friend. And of course, she had not told her parents. What would they all think? She would be in a lot of trouble if anyone found out, and besides, who would want to be around her? There were times when she couldn't stand the hypocritical lifestyle she was leading. But she seemed unable to stop the stealing. Even worse for her was that she didn't know what to do with the stuff once she successfully stole it. She hid it in her room, but she was not sure how long that would be able to continue because by this time she was stealing nearly every day, and there was only so much hiding she could do before her parents would find out. The shame was eating her up. She couldn't face her friends anymore; she didn't want to be around her parents for fear of being found out. Life was miserable, but the only relief seemed to come after she had stolen something—anything. What sense did any of this make?

Signs and Symptoms

The characteristic feature of kleptomania is impulsive stealing. There is a sense of tension before the stealing and a sense of relief afterward. However, a sense of shame and worthlessness accompanies the behavior. Kleptomaniacs typically have many of the following characteristics:

- inability to resist impulses to steal things that are not needed
- stealing that is not related to getting revenge, is not an expression of anger, and is not part of a delusion
- extreme secretiveness about stealing
- stealing that is usually done alone rather than with a friend or other people
- stealing that is not a part of conduct disorder, depression, mania, or the result of chemical use or a dare from others

Kleptomania most commonly begins in midadolescence and continues into the midthirties. There may be periods of no stealing, but the stealing may begin again for no known reason. The exact cause of kleptomania is unknown. Kleptomania tends to be chronic. There is a strong correlation between kleptomania and depression, anxiety disorders, eating disorders, and substance abuse.

Trichotillomania

Trichotillomania (TTM) is characterized by chronic, repetitive pulling of bodily hair. The sites of hair pulling include the scalp, eyelashes, eyebrows, arms, legs, and pubic area. Hair pulling tends to occur in episodes, exacerbated by stress, or sometimes by relaxation (when reading a book or watching television, for example). Often the young person is unaware of pulling her hair. People with TTM experience an increasing sense of tension immediately before pulling out a hair or when attempting to resist hair pulling. When the hair is pulled, they experience immediate feelings of pleasure, gratification, and relief.

Case Study

Monica had begun pulling at her eyebrows at about age twelve. She would pull out most of her eyebrows and then pencil them in so no one would notice. Her parents did know what she was doing, but they didn't know what to do, so they pretty much ignored what they thought was just a bad habit. However, they became alarmed when the eyebrow pulling changed to pulling hair from her head, resulting in huge bald spots that were very obvious. Monica's mother would tell her to quit, and Monica said she would. However, Monica would find herself watching TV and ending up with a pile of hair in her lap. She would also pull her hair when she was anxious, such as at school when taking a test or when homework was difficult. Her friends and teachers noticed but felt helpless to do anything.

Monica tried any number of techniques to quit, but gains she made in a few days would be gone within a few minutes. She was self-conscious at school and was afraid of comments by others. She withdrew from her friends and tended to avoid any school activities. She realized she was pulling her hair to relax, but even when she thought she was relaxed, she ended up pulling her hair. She tried wearing gloves, but that did not work. She tried sitting on her hands, which did not work either. She felt shame that she was out of control and looking very ugly, but she didn't see any solution to her problem. The urge to pull was so strong, the relief after she pulled was so great, but the shame and embarrassment were so encompassing she knew she had to do something.

Signs and Symptoms

Although trichotillomania is listed as an impulse control disorder, it could also be classified as an obsessive compulsive disorder because of the repetitiveness of the behavior. It begins to take on a life of its own, and the person is unable to end the cycle of anxiety, relief, and shame. The young person may attempt to hide the act of pulling, but the consequences are usually quite obvious. Often the young person will try to use scarves or clothing to cover the bare spots. Trichotillomaniacs may display many of the following characteristics:

- recurrent hair pulling, leaving noticeable areas without hair
- an inability to refrain from pulling hair long enough for the hair to grow back to normal lengths
- pleasure, gratification, or relief when pulling out the hair
- significant distress or impairment in social interactions at school or in the family

Young people often start compulsive hair pulling around the ages of twelve or thirteen, although it is not uncommon for it to start at a much younger or older age. Frequently a stressful event can be associated with the onset, such as moving, abuse, family conflict, or the death of a loved one. The symptoms also may be triggered by pubertal hormonal changes. There is no certain cause of trichotillomania. One theory on a biological level is that there is some disruption in the system involving one of the chemical messengers between the nerve cells in parts of the brain. There may be also a combination of factors such as a genetic predisposition and an aggravating stress or circumstance.

Self-Mutilation

Self-mutilation is a common experience among adolescents, particularly girls. Self-mutilation is a repetitive behavior that results in mild to moderate physical injury. Young people who self-mutilate may burn their skin, cut themselves, pick at wounds, or engage in other behaviors that cause physical injury. Most people who self-mutilate use knives, scissors, razor blades, broken glass, pins, belts, fists, and walls. Burns are usually caused by cigarette butts or lighted matches. Self-mutilation follows the pattern of tension before the self-harm, relief following the harm, and shame following the relief.

Case Study

Seventeen-year-old Stephanie had been sexually abused when she was very young. She thought she had gotten over it. Actually what she had done was put the feelings away in a safe place in her mind where they could not be accessed and she could forget about them. She noticed when she got upset she would "numb out" and not have any feelings. It was effective in shutting out any pain, but she wanted to have feelings like happiness or excitement. Now she could not identify any feelings. She had seen a friend cut herself with a razor blade awhile ago. The friend said it didn't hurt and it made her feel alive. Stephanie was reluctant to try it, but when her mother and she had gotten into one more argument about how Stephanie was not doing as well as she could in school, and her mother had yelled at her and told her she was a loser, Stephanie knew what she had to do. She went to the bathroom, locked the door, took a razor blade, and began cutting on her legs. She did not feel any physical pain, which surprised her. She was so angry she kept cutting until there was a pool of blood on the floor. She felt so much calmer. She did not think of anything but the feelings of anger flowing out of her. It worked. She felt relieved. She knew she had a coping mechanism, and she could release her rage and anger from within in a visible and effective way.

Signs and Symptoms

There is no stereotypical person who will choose to mutilate his or her own body, but experts say it's a process that stems from the inability to deal with stress or intense emotions. Symptoms of self-mutilation may include the following:

- strong urges to harm self
- unexplained or frequent injuries
- wearing long pants or long sleeves consistently — even in warm or hot weather
- need for isolation or "being alone"

- presence of bloodstains on the inside of clothing
- credible stories that attempt to explain the wounds, if noticeable

Deliberate self-harm is often found in conjunction with other disorders, such as substance abuse, eating disorders, post-traumatic stress disorder, major depression, anxiety disorders, and schizophrenia.

Response, Diagnosis, and Treatment

None of the impulse control disorders will go away on their own. Some disorders may decrease in intensity or duration for a period of time, but without professional intervention they will most likely return repeatedly. Because shame is such a large factor in each disorder, often the young person will not admit to the impulses but will only tell of symptoms from more acceptable disorders, such as depression or anxiety. The critical action is to let the parents know of concerns you have noticed, recommend professional help, and be supportive of the young person throughout the process, even when it is frustrating and progress is slow.

Impulse control disorders are difficult to treat, and extreme patience is needed in the process. A diagnosis of any of these impulse control disorders can be made only once all other medical and psychiatric disorders that may cause the same symptoms have been ruled out. Experts with each of the disorders may be difficult to find. The disorders are diagnosed by an interview with the young person and her parents. Sometimes the interviews are done with the young person alone, sometimes they include the parents. Questionnaires may be administered to determine the extent of the problems as well as the intensity of the symptoms.

A combination of psychological counseling and medication is the preferred treatment for impulse control disorders. For kleptomania, pyromania, and trichotillomania, behavior modification is usually the treatment of choice. In the case of intermittent explosive disorder, anger management and medication may be used in extreme cases of aggression. Treatment often begins with individual therapy with the young person. With each disorder, some form of education about it is included so the young person will understand the issues around the disorder. From there, depending on the disorder, most likely behavior therapy or cognitive behavior therapy would be initiated. This would involve addressing issues triggering the responses, learning alternative responses, and rewarding positive progress. A form of therapy called dialectical behavior therapy has been found to be effective with self-mutilation. The young person learns skills to cope with overwhelming feelings as well as ways to respect and appreciate one's self. A form of behavior therapy called habit reversal may be used. In this form of therapy, a patient chooses a new action in place of the problem habit. The muscles used to do the new action make it impossible to perform the old habit. For example, patients might tightly squeeze their hands instead of pulling their hair. Relaxation exercises are also recommended. Family therapy may help other family members learn to be supportive of the young person with the disorder and normalize family patterns.

Pastoral Care Strategies

An adult working with youth with impulse control disorders needs to be patient and understanding of the difficulty these young people face in trying to change their behaviors, while at the same time not excusing them or expecting them to fail. Patience with the young person is important, especially when progress is slow.

In your own ministry to and with young people, keep these strategies in mind:

- Keep an open and nonjudgmental mindset about how difficult impulsive control disorders are for young people and their families.
- Work with other churches, schools, and youth-serving organizations to increase public awareness about the importance of protecting and nurturing the mental health of young people.
- Foster recognition that many young people have mental health problems that are real, painful, and sometimes severe.
- Remember that young people with impulse control disorders need a higher level of supervision than other young people of the same age.

- Provide respite and support for parents.
- Develop educational experiences to increase problem-solving abilities in young people.
- Include prayers from the pulpit to comfort those who suffer with a mental illness and their families.
- Encourage good self-care for all young people to prevent or reduce anxiety in difficult situations.
- Advocate for those suffering with mental disorders by participating in the National Day of Prayer for Mental Illness Recovery and Understanding. The day occurs the first Tuesday in October of each year.
- Work with a mental health professional to provide parents with tips on how to strengthen their relationship with their children by spending at least fifteen minutes of daily, undivided time with them and focusing on them.

Recommended Reading

- *A Bright Red Scream: Self-Mutilation and the Language of Pain,* by Marilee Strong (New York: Penguin Books, 1999).
- *The Explosive Child: A New Approach for Understanding and Parenting Easily Frustrated, Chronically Inflexible Children,* by Ross W. Greene (New York: Harper Paperbacks, 2001).
- *Help for Hair Pullers: Understanding and Coping with Trichotillomania,* by Nancy J. Keuthen, PhD; Dan J. Stein; and Gary A. Christensen, MD (Oakland, CA: New Harbinger Publications, 2001).
- *Kleptomania: Ten Stories,* by Manjula Padmanabhan (New York: Penguin Global, 2005).
- *Stop Me Because I Can't Stop Myself: Taking Control of Impulsive Behavior,* by Jon Grant, S. W. Kim, and Gregory Fricchione (New York: McGraw-Hill, 2004).

SECTION FOUR
GRIEF AND LOSS

Young people often handle grief and loss differently from adults. Depending on their age and emotional development, as well as the circumstances of the loss, their grieving process will proceed along a continuum from denial to acceptance. Emotional responses will also vary—from extreme sadness that includes thoughts of suicide and symptoms of post-traumatic stress to temporary feelings of sadness or anxiety. Adolescents are in a unique position developmentally; they are beginning to think about abstract concepts—life and death, the meaning as well as the fragility of life, the lack of permanence of things once thought as unchanging. Young people can run the gamut from feeling responsible for changes in their life, such as their parents' divorce, or feeling guilty for surviving a disaster when others did not.

15
DIVORCE

For many young people, the divorce of their parents marks a turning point in their lives, whether the divorce happened many years ago or is taking place right now. When parents divorce, however, they often do not have the energy to deal with the needs of the children because of the intensity of their own situation. For young people, this can be extremely difficult, or it can be an opportunity to become more independent. Some young people are relieved when their parents finally divorce because of the rancor between the parents for a long time.

Case Study

Jason's parents had been having a difficult time as long as he could remember. He and his younger brothers had often heard them arguing after they had gone to bed. There was tension in the household because there never seemed to be enough money for anything. Jason used to feel like he should be doing something different, but as time went on he decided it really wasn't his responsibility. Now that he was fifteen, all he wanted to do was get out of the house and be with his friends. However, he felt like he should help his brothers, who were five and ten, to cope with his parents' fighting. It never got physically violent, but it was scary for his brothers when there was yelling and name calling.

Last night the parents called their sons together and said they were divorcing. Their dad had left this morning, and everyone was pretty stunned by the news. They had questions about where they were going to live, when they would see their dad, and how they were going to make it financially. Jason had other concerns, however, that he thought were different from his brothers'. He had decided over the years that he was never going to get married because he figured it ended in arguing and fighting and just wasn't worth it. He also thought perhaps he should now look for a job to help out because money was tight before, and now it would be extremely difficult. He also found himself blaming his mom for not being more flexible and being less demanding of his dad. If she would have given in to him more often, they probably wouldn't have been in this predicament to begin with. His dad had previously told him his mother was argumentative and inflexible, and now he could definitely see that was true. More than anything, though, he just wanted to get out of the home and leave everyone else to fend for themselves. He did not want to be the dad when his dad was not around; he did not want to be an adult taking on financial responsibilities. He just wanted to be a kid as long as he could, and that didn't seem like it was going to happen.

Signs and Symptoms

Adolescents tend to have a naïve notion that bad things will not or cannot happen to them. With the divorce rate at about 50 percent, by the time they reach adolescence, most kids will know or befriend someone who is living in a divorced family. This does not mean they will deal with the breakup of their own family any better. Symptoms of adjustment to divorce may include the following:

- decreased school performance
- withdrawal from family and friends
- increased time with friends
- increased interest in risk-taking behaviors, such as drugs, alcohol, and sex
- sadness, feeling lost and alone
- disinterest in activities that were once enjoyable
- anxiety about day-to-day events
- concerns about adult matters
- regression to previous developmental levels
- decreased interest in eating
- change in sleeping habits
- inability to concentrate
- anger and irritability
- frequent mood changes
- talk about running away or wanting to die
- evidence of self-harm

It's common for teens to think that their parents' divorce is somehow their fault, but nothing could be further from the truth. Some teens may wonder if they could have helped prevent the split. Others may wish they had prevented arguments by cooperating more within the family. But separation and divorce are a result of a couple's problems with each other, not with their kids. The decisions adults make about divorce are their own. Many times parents will put their children in the middle of the divorce, leaving adolescents wondering whether to help out or check out. Adolescents understand what is happening in a divorce better than younger children do and have more resources available to them, but that does not mean they will cope with the changes any better than children.

Response, Diagnosis, and Treatment

Even if a divorce in a family seems to have been inevitable and anticipated, when it actually happens, the young person may act as though it was entirely unexpected. When the dynamics of the family change, there is a great deal of uncertainty of the future. Familiarity, even if it was uncomfortable, is no longer present. Support for the feelings of the young person, no matter how they are expressed, needs to be available within appropriate limits. When the emotional responses are extreme and unhealthy, it is good to let one or both parents know about the concerns and to recommend professional help. The professional diagnosis is based on how the young person is responding to the divorce. Possible diagnoses might include adjustment disorder with anxiety, depression, or disturbance of conduct. Treatment consists of allowing the youth to talk about his concerns, fears, and feelings. The therapist would work with one or both parents to prevent having the young person placed in the middle of the divorce, having to take sides, or having to take on adult responsibilities. If this were not possible, the young person would be educated in ways to deal with his parents so he would be able to maintain healthy limits with them and remain close to both of them. In extreme cases, where a divorce occurs because of violence or chemical abuse, maintaining the safety of the children becomes primary. Support groups are also an excellent means of helping youth to work out their emotions and learn they are not alone.

Pastoral Care Strategies

Young people can be adept at hiding their feelings and may not be interested in letting others know what is happening in their lives. On the other hand, they may be ready to accept outside help from trusted adults. In either case, it is important to be available to the youth, set appropriate limits with them, and encourage them to make healthy choices for themselves.

In your own ministry to and with young people, keep these strategies in mind:

- Be present to all family members dealing with divorce without being intrusive into their lives.
- Offer space for support groups for youth with separated or divorced parents.
- If you know other young people who are dealing with divorce (or have dealt with it), arrange for them to spend time together.

- Remain nonjudgmental and avoid talking poorly about either parent of a young person, even if the young person has negative things to say.
- Teach parents how and why to avoid putting children in the middle of negotiations and conflicts.
- Create an online support group for kids dealing with divorce, to offer peer support and networking.
- Create a survival kit for families, which includes written information about children and divorce, do's and don'ts, and stories and prayers of encouragement.
- Develop a reference and lending library of books, tapes, videos, and workbooks that focus on divorce, good parenting, communication skills, and so on. Make these resources available for browsing or borrowing.
- Invite divorced parents to speak with newly divorced or divorcing parents about how to handle transitions with their family. You might even consider creating a mentoring program among parents.
- Work with a local mental health professional or family service organization to establish a program for separating or divorced parents to assist them in helping their children cope with and successfully manage the stress of parental divorce.

Recommended Reading

- *Dear Mom and Dad: What Kids of Divorce Really Want to Say to Their Parents*, by Gillian Rothchild (New York: Pocket Books, 1999).
- *Difficult Questions Kids Ask and Are Afraid to Ask About Divorce*, by Joan Zuckerberg and Meg F. Schneider (New York: Fireside Publishing, 1996).
- *The Divorce Helpbook for Teens*, by Cynthia MacGregor (Atascadero, CA: Impact Publishers, 2004).

16
DISASTERS

Disasters are events out of the range of normal experiences and are likely to affect many people in a community and surrounding areas. Disasters include events such as floods, tornadoes, terrorist attacks, violence, hurricanes, fires, and earthquakes. Generally the closer the individual is to the disaster, the more intense the response. The age of the person, strength of the support system, emotional health of the individual and the family, extent of the damage, and availability of community resources all determine the effects of a disaster on an individual.

Case Study

Natalie was thirteen when a tornado ripped through her community. She thought she and her family were prepared. They had a designated safe place in their home—they had a family plan for shelter. She knew when the tornado warnings were given that the family would go to the safe place. What she was not prepared for, however, was what to do after the tornado struck. She, her parents, and her two younger brothers were huddled in a closet with no windows. They heard the shrill sound, like a train passing over them. They also heard the unimaginable sounds of heavy objects being tossed around like toys. They heard what sounded like their house being blown away around them. Then they heard the silence. That was probably the scariest part because it was so eerily quiet. They left their closet to find destruction and devastation all around them. Their house was damaged beyond their wildest imaginings. Their neighborhood was destroyed, with others' homes reduced to rubble, piles of lumber, and possessions strewn in all directions. They could not begin to think about what to do now. Natalie would not be able to describe her feelings for some time. She was grateful she and her family were alive, but beyond that she was stunned and overwhelmed. She and her parents clung to the younger children and stared and wondered at the losses in front of them. They were aware it was raining heavily and they should do something or go somewhere, but where and how?

Signs and Symptoms

A sign of distress is an abrupt or significant change in behavior or attitude of the person experiencing the distress. These changes can be dramatic or subtle. They can be long- or short-term. They can vary in degree or intensity. A disaster will most often trigger signs of distress like these:

- fear and anxiety
- sleep disturbances
- withdrawal and isolation
- physical complaints such as headaches and stomachaches
- depression and sadness
- aggressive behavior, such as stealing, acting out, verbal attacks
- poor academic performance
- alcohol and drug use
- unwillingness to separate from parents or family

- regression to previous behaviors, such as thumb sucking, rocking, bed-wetting
- detachment, shame, and guilt
- difficulty concentrating
- questioning of spiritual beliefs
- inability to process the significance of the event
- phobias, health concerns
- crying easily
- change in appetite
- repeatedly talking about the event
- refusal to go to school
- fatigue

("Typical Reactions of Children," National Mental Health Information Center Web site)

Distress reactions to disasters are usually temporary, with most young people returning to normal functioning within a few weeks. However, if the person does not return to former functioning within a short time, professional treatment may be necessary.

Response, Diagnosis, and Treatment

When working with young people who have experienced a disaster, it is important to keep their developmental needs in mind, particularly their need for emerging independence and a sense of control over their environment. It is also important not to minimize their responses to a disaster, even though they may not have been immediately involved. Of utmost importance is communication with the youths' parents to inform them of your concerns. If the parents are unable to manage their own stress and the stress of their children, let them know where the family can get professional help.

Young people may seem to want to cope on their own and may appear to reject help from others because they want to assert their independence and not appear weak or inadequate. Provide an opportunity for them to talk, emphasize the normalcy of their responses, and assure them they are not responsible for the effects of the disaster. They may need encouragement to talk to their parents and friends about their feelings to get a sense of not being alone and not being abnormal. Professional help is needed when the young person does not return to normal functioning within a few weeks.

Diagnosis of problems with integrating the effects of the disaster is correlated with the extent of the difficulties. Treatment consists of providing a safe place for the person to talk about the feelings that accompany memories of the disaster. If necessary, medications might be prescribed to relieve either anxiety or depression. Group therapy is used when there are many people with similar concerns who could benefit from listening to others and sharing their feelings.

Pastoral Care Strategies

When disaster strikes, a young person's view of the world as a safe and predictable place is temporarily lost. Children become afraid that the event will happen again and they or their family may be injured or killed. The damage, injuries, and deaths that can result from an unexpected or uncontrollable event are difficult for most young people to understand. Strong support from a parent or other adult following any traumatic event can help children recover more quickly and completely.

In your own ministry to and with young people, keep these strategies in mind:

- Find out about local support groups for those who have suffered from disasters. These can be especially helpful for people with limited personal support systems.
- Encourage young people and families to do something positive that will help them gain a greater sense of control (for example, give blood, take a first aid class, or donate food or clothing).
- Create some planned activities in response to a disaster, such as a candlelight vigil, benefit, discussion group, or special lecture.
- Suggest parents monitor media exposure to a disastrous event, including information received on the Internet.
- Provide care packages or simple meals to families dealing with a disaster.

- Hold meetings for parents to discuss the traumatic event, their children's response to it, and how they and you can help. Involve mental health professionals in these meetings if possible.
- Educate youth about the necessity of self-care when a disaster has occurred in order to manage the stress that accompanies the disaster.
- Stay as connected as possible to young people if they are moved to other areas because of a disaster.
- Create rituals. Rituals can help the family in the healing process and reaffirm family bonds. As an example, one family who lost their home in a fire filled balloons, each representing something they lost in the fire. The family gathered in a circle at the site of their home and said a few words about what each item meant and then released the balloons into the air.
- Hold listening sessions with young people. These sessions can be useful in letting young people know their fears and concerns are normal reactions. Involve mental health professionals in these activities if possible.
- Help families create a family disaster plan or replenish essential disaster supplies in case a disaster happens again. The American Red Cross encourages five key actions: make a plan, build a kit, get trained, volunteer, and give blood.
- Encourage young people to develop coping and problem-solving skills as well as age-appropriate methods for managing anxiety.

Recommended Reading

- *Dealing with Disasters: Teaching About Disasters for 11–14-Year-Olds,* by Teresa Garlake and Rebecca Sudworth (Oxford, England: Oxfam Publishing, 2000).
- *Helping Children Cope with Stress,* by Avis Brenner (New York: Jossey-Bass, 1997).
- *Raising Our Children to Be Resilient: A Guide to Helping Children Cope with Trauma in Today's World,* by Linda Goldman (New York: Brunner-Routledge, 2004).

17
SUICIDE

"Suicide is the willful taking of one's life. It is the third leading cause of death for 15- to 24-year-olds and the sixth leading cause of death for 5- to 14-year-olds" (Mental Health Association of Westchester Web site). The primary cause of suicide is an untreated mental illness, such as depression, bipolar disorder, or schizophrenia. Negative experiences increase the likelihood of depression and suicide. These negative experiences might include loss of a loved one; loss of a job; breakup of a relationship; serious illness; chronic pain; physical, emotional, or sexual abuse; feelings of hopeless and helplessness; alcohol or drug abuse, low self-esteem; and being bullied.

Case Study

When he was fifteen, Christopher was fun to be around. He was willing to try new adventures and enjoyed being with people. His mother had bouts of depression; his dad was a recovering alcoholic. His mother was able to manage her depression with medication, and it was not a serious problem at this time in Chris's life. His dad had quit drinking when Chris was born so that was no longer an issue either. Therefore Chris was surprised when he began feeling alienated from his family. And he was not interested in doing things with his friends. Everything around him lacked color and seemed to be a universal gray. He did not want to participate in school activities. Most days it was a chore to get up and go to school. Once he was there, he had difficulty concentrating. When his grades went down, he became more despondent. He didn't know what to do about it all and withdrew more and more into his room. One night he decided there was no use in continuing and decided to end his life. The pain was unremitting and there seemed to be no hope of change. His mother had taken him to a doctor a couple weeks before, and he was on medication but nothing seemed to be changing. He called his friend Zach and said he wanted to die. He had found an old hunting gun of his dad's and was going to use it to kill himself. Zach talked to Chris for a while, but Chris did not seem to change his mind. When Chris hung up on him, Zach told his mother about the conversation. His mother called Chris's mother and told her what Chris had told Zach. Chris's mother went to the garage and was alarmed when she saw the gun in Chris's hands. She got the gun away from him and immediately drove him to the hospital.

Signs and Symptoms

Thinking about suicide goes beyond normal ideas young people may have about death and life. Wishing to be dead, thinking about suicide, or feeling helpless and hopeless about how to solve life's problems are signs that a young person may be at risk and in need of help and support. Additional symptoms of suicidal thinking may include the following:

- depression
- impulsivity
- previous suicide attempts
- withdrawal from usual activities and people

- threats of suicide
- statements about wanting to die
- giving away favorite things
- untreated bipolar disorder or schizophrenia
- sudden change from depression to happy mood
- self-mutilation

Suicide attempts are usually made when a person is seriously depressed or upset. A teen feeling suicidal may see no other way out of problems, no other escape from emotional pain, or no other way to communicate his desperate unhappiness.

Response, Diagnosis, and Treatment

No talk of suicide should be taken lightly. Any suicidal gesture, no matter how "harmless" it seems, demands immediate professional attention. If you suspect suicidal thoughts or behavior, ask the young person directly if he is considering suicide. Don't avoid the subject or wait for the young person to come to you. Most of the time young people who are considering suicide are willing to discuss it if someone asks them out of concern and care. Don't argue with the person or make statements like, "It's not as bad as you think." Don't challenge the person by saying, "You're not the type to commit suicide." Arguing with the person may only increase his feelings of being out of control of his life.

Talk about the situation as openly as possible. Tell the person you don't want him to die or to harm another person. Show understanding and compassion. Never agree to keep the discussion of suicide with a young person a secret; parents must be informed and professional help must be sought immediately.

The treatment for suicidal thoughts might range from professional counseling to admission to the hospital. Effective treatment includes medications, counseling, and development of coping strategies and an action plan to follow when symptoms reappear. If the person's suicidal thoughts are believed to be of a dangerous nature, follow-up is likely to be immediate, with admission to the hospital. If someone is admitted to the hospital because of suicidal thoughts, he undergoes extensive evaluation by a psychiatrist and often is started on medication and scheduled for follow-up counseling.

Pastoral Care Strategies

Because young people aren't always able to understand and explain their feelings, as adults we must be more vigilant in understanding the ways depression and suicide manifest in children, and work to get them the help they need. In your own ministry to and with young people, keep these strategies in mind:

- Believe any young person who threatens suicide or says he wants to die.
- Educate yourself about the problem of youth suicide and the tools of prevention.
- When a suicide does occur in the community, conduct listening sessions with young people and their parents. Involve mental health professionals in these activities if possible.
- Talk about suicide in an open manner. Young people need to be given a chance to discuss suicide by voicing their thoughts and opinions. Candid discussion is particularly important when a suicide has occurred in the local community.
- Let young people know about suicide hotline telephone numbers and crisis intervention services that are accessible locally.
- Model healthy behavior and positive problem-solving approaches. Adults can be models for young people by dealing with their own stress in a constructive manner.
- Use TV shows, films, newspaper articles, and other media as triggers for discussion of effective ways to deal with stress and depression.
- Provide opportunities for group support. Young people can benefit from sharing problems with other young people who help them find solutions.
- Learn about creating and implementing suicide prevention programs.
- Sponsor an annual Suicide Prevention Week in your community.

- Sponsor a community-wide petition to encourage legislators to get involved in the prevention of youth suicide.
- Sponsor a poster campaign for your school or church community on the awareness and prevention of youth suicide.

Recommended Reading

- *The Power to Prevent Suicide: A Guide for Teens Helping Teens*, by Richard E. Nelson, PhD, and Judith C. Galas (Minneapolis: Free Spirit Publishing, 1994).
- *Suicide: The Forever Decision: For Those Thinking About Suicide, and for Those Who Know, Love, or Counsel Them*, by Paul G. Quinnett (New York: Crossroads Publishing, 1987).
- *Why Suicide? Answers to 200 of the Most Frequently Asked Questions About Suicide*, by Eric Marcus (San Francisco: HarperSanFrancisco, 1996).

18
DEATH AND DYING

Death comes into our lives at all ages. Grief and mourning are part of the natural order of living. Children and young people may begin the grief process with the death of their pets. Sometimes they have unexpected tragedies occur and are unable to manage the coping strategies required to grieve in a healthy manner. Death is not something we are generally comfortable talking about. It is not usually a topic on the minds of young people. When the death of a loved one occurs, it is often difficult for the young person as well as the people around her. It is important to be present to the young person and consider her needs in the process of grieving.

Case Study

Olivia was twelve when her mother was diagnosed with breast cancer. She was the youngest of three children and the only girl in the family. Her brothers were close to their mother but had begun the process of separating from her as they entered mid- and late adolescence. Olivia was sure her mother would be fine and wanted to stay close to her at all times. When her mother was told the

146

cancer was serious and treatment needed to be begun immediately, Olivia remained optimistic. Everything seemed fine for about a year or so.

By the time Olivia was thirteen, her thoughts of her mother's cancer had all but disappeared. Then she noticed that her mother was getting more tired, less interested in doing things with Olivia. Olivia wanted answers to questions she had, but no one seemed to be talking to her, including her mother. Her dad was of little help; he seemed to be unwilling to talk about her mother at all. Olivia realized her mother was not well when she returned to the hospital for several weeks. She also realized her mother was not going to recover when hospice volunteers began coming to the house after her mother was discharged from the hospital. Her brothers were spending a lot of time at home, which was unusual. Her dad was quiet and withdrawn. Olivia was unsure where to go to talk with someone.

Eventually Olivia's mother died, and Olivia felt numb about the events following her mother's death. She went through the rituals and talked to people who came to the funeral, burial, and their home. She did not cry, however, because she wanted to stay strong like her brothers and dad. In her room at night, she would allow herself to cry herself to sleep, would have dreams about dying, and would be afraid to go to sleep. She missed her mother terribly and wished she would come back just to say good-bye one more time, have one more hug and kiss, and tell Olivia she loved her.

Signs and Symptoms

Most of the time, young people get through the grieving process without difficulty. They are able to express their emotions and get support from their friends and family. In cases of tragedy, suicide, or death of a parent or close family member, the young person may be less able to grieve in a healthy manner. It is important to notice the signs and symptoms of unhealthy grieving or a lack of grieving in these young people. Symptoms of unhealthy grieving may include the following:

- inability to accept death has occurred
- frequent nightmares and intrusive memories
- constant desire to be with the deceased
- withdrawal from others
- suicidal thoughts
- uncontrollable crying
- continual thoughts of death
- feelings of hopelessness or worthlessness
- deteriorating ability to function, even in everyday activities
- increased anger, hostility, and irritability
- decreased school performance
- overactivity, constant busyness
- drug or alcohol abuse
- significant loss or gain of weight
- self-destructive or criminal behavior
- promiscuity

Adolescents and young people generally respond similarly to adults but may have more intensity in their responses. They tend to need peers more when they are grieving than adults do. They may also be less willing to talk and need to do more experiential activities.

Response, Diagnosis, and Treatment

When a parent, sibling, friend, or relative dies, a young person feels the overwhelming loss of someone who helped shape her fragile self-identity. And these feelings about the death become a part of her life forever.

Caring adults—whether parents, teachers, youth ministers, counselors, or friends—can help young people during this time. If adults are open, honest, and loving, experiencing the loss of someone loved can be a chance for young people to learn about both the joy and the pain that come from caring deeply for others.

Unfortunately many adults discourage young people from sharing their grief. Bereaved young people give out all kinds of signs they are struggling with complex feelings, yet are often pressured to act as if they are doing better than they really are.

To help a young person having a particularly hard time with her loss, explore the full spectrum of helping services in your community. School counselors and private therapists are appropriate resources for some young people, whereas others may just need a little more time and attention from caring adults. Young people need caring adults to confirm that it's all right to be sad and to feel a multitude of emotions when someone they love dies.

Professional help is usually needed only when extreme signs of grieving have been going on for an extended period of time. Peer support groups are one of the best ways to help bereaved young people heal. In many cases, grief therapy is also beneficial. In the immediate aftermath of the death, the bereaved struggling with grief-related symptoms may also benefit from coaching in symptom-management techniques, such as relaxation skills.

Pastoral Care Strategies

In working with young people who are grieving the loss of a significant person in their lives, it is important to normalize their feelings, help them accept the loss and express their feelings, and help them be aware that grieving does not mean they will forget the person or their importance in their lives. In your own ministry to and with young people, keep these strategies in mind:

- Share your own personal experiences with death. Young people are able to relate better if you discuss how you felt when your grandmother died when you were an adolescent or how you lost a friend in a car accident.
- Offer opportunities for young people to discuss openly the variety of feelings and emotions they may experience when someone or something dies.
- Provide young people and families with the materials to create a special photo album or memory book.

- Discuss customs regarding death observed by other cultures to enhance young people's ability to understand the reactions of peers of diverse backgrounds.
- Anticipate and prepare for future rough spots. An assignment to draw a family tree, the first Mother's Day after a death, an upcoming Christmas, even a graduation a few years down the road are just some of the potential triggers that may pose new challenges for young people.
- Encourage expression in private ways, such as through journals or art. Consider providing young people with materials for this type of expression.
- Offer to take care of pets while the family is busy with funeral activities, invite peers or parishioners to send cards to the family, or donate to a special cause in the family's name.
- Teach young people techniques to calm themselves. Offer them the opportunity to relax through play, talk, art activities, or music. Exercise, muscle relaxation techniques, deep-breathing exercises, and using calm mental images are techniques proven to reduce stress.
- Be available. Letting young people (and family members) know you are available for whatever is needed — be it a late-night phone call, a ride to a doctor's appointment, or company for a movie — can give them peace of mind.
- Ask what needs to be done or look around to discover what might be needed. There is no end to the ways others can be of service. And if you have a particular expertise, offer to share it. Someone with an extra bedroom can offer out-of-town relatives a place to stay, for example.
- Avoid clichés. Although they are well meaning, many people recite phrases they have heard that may sound hollow or untrue. Saying, "You'll be fine," "You're strong," "It's for the best," "Time heals all wounds," or "I know how you feel" negate the person's strong feelings.
- Maintain ongoing contact with young people, even when they seem disinterested.
- In ways that are personally meaningful for the bereaved, encourage memorialization (rituals) of someone who died.

- Offer the opportunity for young people to talk about topics around death when it is not a time of crisis.

Recommended Reading

- *The Grieving Teen: A Guide for Teenagers and Their Friends*, by Helen Fitzgerald (Wichita, KS: Fireside, 2000).
- *Healing Your Grieving Heart for Teens*, by Alan D. Wolfelt, PhD (Laguna Hills, CA: Companion Press, 2001).
- *Helping Children Cope with the Loss of a Loved One: A Guide for Grownups*, by William C. Kroen and Pamela Espeland (Minneapolis: Free Spirit Publishing, 1996).
- *Helping Teens Work Through Grief*, by Mary K. Perschy (London: Taylor and Francis, 2004).

APPENDIX

A Crisis Intervention Approach

A nonprofessional pastoral response to young people should be guided by the following principles:

- Listen twice as much as you talk when assisting young people and families in crisis. The most essential skill for caregiving is genuine listening.
- Help guide the decision-making process. Resist the temptation to solve problems, to rescue, or to become a font of advice.
- Express and receive honest emotions. Allow individuals to vent the feelings that may have been bottled up inside by listening in a nonjudgmental manner and asking clarifying questions to assist them in accurately naming their emotions.
- Extend realistic hope amid a crisis. Enable young people and parents in crisis to gain perspective in a situation that may seem overwhelming and confusing. By assisting young people (and parents) in naming their problems, identifying possible solutions, discovering possible resources and supports, and expressing their feelings, you can bring hope. That hope, however, must be realistic.

Make Contact

The first step includes either the young person (or parents) coming to you and asking for advice or assistance, or you going to the young person (or his parents) because you perceive an issue. When you have to make the initial contact, it is important for you to identify the observable behaviors that have caused concern. Anchor your concern in observable behavior.

Dealing with Parents Who Are in Denial

Unfortunately many parents will immediately deny that their young person is in trouble. Be sure to remain calm and maintain your composure. A calm response will often help defuse a potentially volatile situation. Here are some other helpful strategies:

- If you are sitting behind your desk, move your chair out and place it close to the parents. You will send an assertive message of being comfortable with the situation.
- Maintain eye contact. This is the most effective technique in dealing with defensive or denying parents.
- Your body language should express an attitude that is pleasant, not defensive, and it should show parents you are interested in the well-being of their child. Be sure to focus on the one common denominator in the conversation—care for the young person. Keep the conversation focused on the young person and what is best for him.
- Show empathy and understanding as you listen. Try to imagine yourself walking in the parents' shoes, so you can gain an understanding of their feelings.
- Address only the specific concerns you have. Do not discuss other issues that might be important but unrelated to the immediate concern. Focus on what you and the parent can do together to solve the problem.
- If the conference is going nowhere, find a graceful way to conclude it. This will allow parents the time they may need to think through your concerns. Be sure to let parents know you are available for further conversation, support, and referral.

Gather Information

Let the young person (or parents) tell her story if it's an individual crisis. Ask good clarifying questions and use effective reflective listening skills. That is an essential step in "naming" the problem accurately.

Define confidentiality before any one-on-one conversations and explain the limits of confidentiality. Confidentiality never applies when there is a possibility of a young person hurting himself, hurting another person, or being hurt by someone else. In addition, young people must never be told they cannot disclose any portion of a conversation (including behaviors) between themselves and an adult.

Explore Solutions

In this step, brainstorm the possible responses to the issue and identify potential consequences. Your role is to facilitate the young person's (or parents') problem solving, rather than to provide advice. By enabling the young person or parents to identify a response, ownership is created for the solution because it is their solution, not yours. At this point, if you are dealing directly with a young person, you will need to invite the parents to enter into the conversation.

Develop a Plan

Assist the young person and his parents in identifying the concrete steps that might be taken. The steps should be simple, specific, doable, and short-term actions that include who will do what, when, where, and how. Regardless of whether the issue is a family, school, personal, or relationship issue, practical action steps with a realistic timeline are essential.

For serious issues, the plan will often involve referral to a professional or a community resource.

Follow Up

Set a time for meeting together again to evaluate the action steps. This builds in accountability and assures the young person and her parents that you are committed to providing ongoing support.

(Adapted from McCarty, ed., *The Vision of Catholic Youth Ministry*, pp. 156–158)

ACKNOWLEDGMENTS

The definitions of *addiction* and *addict* on page 11 are from *Merriam-Webster's Collegiate Dictionary,* eleventh edition (Springfield, MA: Merriam-Webster, 2004), page 14. Copyright © 2004 by Merriam-Webster.

The quotation about substance abuse on page 14, the information about PTSD symptoms on page 102, the information about OCD symptoms on page 106, and the information on impulse-control disorders on page 117 are based on and from *Diagnostic and Statistical Manual of Mental Disorders,* fourth edition, by DSM-IV-TR™ (Washington, DC: American Psychiatric Association, 2000), pages 199, 466, 460, and 663, respectively. Copyright © 2000 by the American Psychiatric Association.

The bulleted items on page 27 are based on "The Range of Teenage Sexual Behavior," at the Focus Adolescent Services Web site, *www.focusas.com/SexualBehavior.html,* accessed May 17, 2006.

The quotation on page 43 is from the Safe Child Web site, by the Coalition for Children, *www.safechild.org/childabuse1.htm,* accessed May 17, 2006.

The bulleted list on pages 45–46 is from *Creating Safe and Sacred Places: Identifying, Preventing, and Healing Sexual Abuse,* by Gerard J. McGlone and Mary Shrader with Laurie Delgatto (Winona, MN: Saint Mary's Press, 2003), pages 30–31. Copyright © 2003 by Saint Mary's Press. All rights reserved.

The statistics on the rate of sexual abuse on page 46 are from "Stop It Now!" The Campaign to Prevent Child Sexual Abuse Web site, *www.stopitnow.org/asit_epidemic.html,* accessed May 17, 2006.

The statistics on child sexual assaults on page 46 are from the Love Our Children USA Web site, *www.loveourchildrenusa.org/sexualabuse.php,* accessed May 17, 2006.

The definitions and statistics on pages 50 and 50–51 are from the National Exchange Club Foundation Web sites, *www.preventchildabuse.com/emotion.htm* and *www.preventchildabuse.com/physical.htm,* accessed May 17, 2006.

The statistic on teenage dating on page 58 is from the "Teen Dating

Violence" fact sheet, at the National Center for Victims of Crime Web site, *www.ncvc.org*, accessed May 17, 2006.

The bulleted items in "Signs and Symptoms" on pages 105 and 106 are from the Obsessive-Compulsive Foundation Web site, *www. ocfoundation.org/what-is-ocd.htm*, accessed May 17, 2006.

The bulleted items on pages 137–138 are based on "Typical Reactions of Children," at the National Mental Health Information Center Web site, *www.mentalhealth.samhsa.gov/publications/allpubs/ ADM86-1070/chapter2.asp*, accessed May 17, 2006.

The quotation on page 141 is from the Mental Health Association of Westchester Web site, *www.mhawestchester.org/diagnosechild/ suicidec.asp*, accessed May 17, 2006.

"A Crisis Intervention Approach" on pages 153–155 is adapted from *The Vision of Catholic Youth Ministry: Fundamentals, Theory, and Practice*, edited by Robert McCarty (Winona, MN: Saint Mary's Press, 2005), pages 156–158. Copyright © 2005 by Saint Mary's Press. All rights reserved.

To view copyright terms and conditions for Internet materials cited here, log on to the home pages for the referenced Web sites.

During this book's preparation, all citations, facts, figures, names, addresses, telephone numbers, Internet URLs, and other pieces of information cited within were verified for accuracy. The authors and Saint Mary's Press staff have made every attempt to reference current and valid sources, but we cannot guarantee the content of any source, and we are not responsible for any changes that may have occurred since our verification. If you find an error in, or have a question or concern about, any of the information or sources listed within, please contact Saint Mary's Press.

As awareness and education increase concerning children and the mental health issues they face, this book is a timely and excellent resource for those teachers and ministers who work directly with youth.

Helping Kids in Crisis: Recognize, Respond, Refer is a practical as well as informational guide with identification and ideas to meet the needs of our youth today that struggle with mental health issues.

I strongly recommend this book as it can enhance a teacher or minister's capacity to reach out and help those youth affected by mental illness.

—Lori Kuenn, MA, LP